In this excellent book, Da   ho feels
trapped and in need of relational change how to experience a break-
through. His message is compelling, practical, hope-filled, and inspi-
rational. His nine options for relational change are life transforming.

—JIM BURNS, PH.D.
President, HomeWord
Author of *Confident Parenting* and *Closer*

Healthy relationships. We all want them, but sometimes we feel trapped
in our interactions with friends and family. What are your options?
Daniel Nehrbass reminds us that the answer might be more simple
than we think. From his real-world perch, interacting with hundreds
of clients, Daniel reminds us there are only nine possible responses to
choose when relationships frustrate us. Dive into learning and bring
your relationships to a place of freedom, openness, and trust.

—GREG LEITH,
Chief Executive Officer, Convene

We humans subconsciously try to change other people, especially
when we feel frustrated, helpless, or trapped. A classic irony is that
nearly everyone comes for counseling help in their relationships
with the expectation and desire that the other person(s) change! Dan
Nehrbass both understands and helps us with this futile and foolish
temptation. In his powerful guide to personal freedom and relational
health, Untrapped: Nine Secrets to Getting Along, Dr. Nehrbass provides us with Biblically grounded and psychologically sound advice
which is tangible, practical, and effective. If you internalize and apply

these liberating and life-changing principles, you will revolutionize and redeem your relationships!

—REV. JARED PINGLETON, PSY.D.
Minister/Clinical Psychologist, Author of *Making Magnificent Marriages,* co-author of *Be Strong and Surrender: A 30 Day Recovery Guide,* and *The Struggle is Real: How to Minister to Mental and Relational Health Needs in the Church.* Vice-President, American Association of Christian Counselors

UN
TRAPPED

Nine Secrets to Getting Along

Daniel Nehrbass, Ph.D.

AMBASSADOR INTERNATIONAL
GREENVILLE, SOUTH CAROLINA & BELFAST, NORTHERN IRELAND

www.ambassador-international.com

UnTrapped
Nine Secrets to Getting Along
©2017 by Daniel Nehrbass, Ph.D.
All rights reserved

ISBN: 978-1-62020-586-0
eISBN: 978-1-62020-663-8

Cover Design and Page Layout by Hannah Nichols
eBook Conversion by Anna Riebe Raats

AMBASSADOR INTERNATIONAL
Emerald House
411 University Ridge, Suite B14
Greenville, SC 29601, USA
www.ambassador-international.com

AMBASSADOR BOOKS
The Mount
2 Woodstock Link
Belfast, BT6 8DD, Northern Ireland, UK
www.ambassadormedia.co.uk

The colophon is a trademark of Ambassador

Dedicated to my six children: the success I wish most for you is in your relationships.

CONTENTS

INTRODUCTION

MARIE, WHO IS A GOOD friend of mine, recently came to me with a difficult dilemma. She lives with her mother and sister. Her mother has a condition that many people nowadays refer to as hoarding—a behavior which stems from an anxiety disorder. Because her mother's behavior is atypical, Marie's home life naturally includes many atypical challenges.

One of the most frustrating issues she faces is the cleanliness of the bathroom. As a hoarder, her mother doesn't see the way the bathroom appears to most people. The deteriorating condition doesn't bother her, but it does bother Marie.

Now Marie has a tough decision to make. If she cleans the bathroom, she enables her mother to continue living without practicing proper hygiene, and she will resent her mother for not helping. But if she doesn't clean the bathroom, she will have to suffer with its condition. And refusing to clean the room would begin a showdown that she will probably lose because she will end up cleaning the bathroom before her mother does.

Since I am a professional Christian counselor, Marie asked me what I thought she should do. I am often tempted to supply an immediate answer that fixes the problem and impresses my friend with a simple solution. But this conundrum stumped me. On the one hand, I could not think of any particular right answer. On the other hand, I could imagine several possible choices that all had their advantages. In a sense, I felt torn among several good possibilities. But even among all these viable options, I could not envision a course of action that would necessarily result in her mother cleaning the bathroom. Yet I could envision multiple options that would result in a happier Marie.

I brainstormed with Marie about her positive options for change. We wrote a list of possibilities on my whiteboard and came up with the chart below. (Each of these options will be explored in the following chapters, but here is a quick overview.)

- **Teach**. Marie could tell her mom, "Our bathroom is not sanitary. Typically, people keep their bathrooms cleaner than this." Or, after cleaning the bathroom, she could say, "This is the type of bathroom I am comfortable living with."

- **Appeal**. Marie could make an emotional connection with her mother by saying something like, "I feel uncomfortable with the way our bathroom is kept." Or she could say, "I feel you are taking advantage of me because it seems like I am doing the majority of the work keeping our bathroom clean."

- **Listen**. Marie could make an empathic connection and try to see the bathroom the way her mother does. She could ask, "Mom, how do you feel about our bathroom? When I ask you to help clean it, what thought goes through your mind? What would it mean to you if I said that I was not going to help clean it anymore?"

- **Sacrifice.** Marie could make an intentional decision to clean the bathroom by herself, without complaining. She could determine that this is an act of love and a practical way to follow Christ's example of sacrifice.

- **Do nothing.** This may sound unappealing, but it is certainly an option. What makes it worthy of consideration is that sometimes doing nothing is a valuable way to teach or to learn. If Marie decides not to clean the bathroom, at least she will not resent her mother for taking advantage of her, and she will not be enabling her mother to live without consequences.

- **Leave.** Marie could move out. She may determine that cleaning the bathroom creates too much resentment for her and perpetuates the cycle of her enabling her mother's behavior. And she may decide that doing nothing is also unacceptable. If she can't live with a messy bathroom and resents cleaning it herself, maybe she will have to live somewhere else.

- **Make a boundary.** Marie could make a boundary with her mother. She could say, "I am willing to clean the bathroom twice a month. I would like you to help me at least one of these times. If you are not willing to help, I will deduct $50 from my rent." Or she could say, "We have two bathrooms in this house. I am willing to clean one of them. If you are not willing to help clean it, I would like you to use the other one."

- **Compromise.** Marie could work out an arrangement with her mother, where both offer something and give up something. In order to do this, she will probably have to do some of the listening mentioned previously and maybe even make some boundaries. But through this conversation, perhaps they could reach a compromise. She may even add some sacrifice to this compromise and not expect a 50/50 arrangement. Marie could offer to clean the bathroom three times a month and ask her mother to do it once a month.

- **Repent**. Marie could address this problem by taking responsibility for her own sin. Perhaps she has resented her mother, and this has bred contempt or hatred. Marie could confess this sin and repent of it. Maybe Marie has played the victim, rather than being straightforward with her mother. It could be that her anger has been disproportionate to the actual situation, and she has treated her mother unfairly. Maybe the cleanliness of the bathroom has become too important to her and now serves as an idol of sorts. In either case, this soul-searching is sure to help the relationship and to restore Marie's own sense of peace about the crisis.

WILL IT WORK?

When Marie and I brainstormed about these nine positive options for change, she evaluated each one with the question, "Will it work?" The answer to that question depends, of course, upon what result she is trying to achieve. Most likely, she is looking for a single, simple outcome—her mother will start helping to clean the bathroom.

Any of the nine options for relational change could effect this change. I cannot predict with certainty which will be most effective. With more information, we might be able to make a case for why one option is better than another. (For instance, if we know that Marie has already tried a thousand emotional appeals, she should probably try something different today.) But each option has its advantage and is effective in its own way. Here's how.

- **Teach**. Maybe in the past Marie has primarily tried emotional appeals. Perhaps her mother feels humiliated when Marie tells her she feels frustrated or disgusted. It could be that the emotional appeal is so difficult for her mother to hear, she is unable to reflect on the situation. If Marie tells her mother, "Our bathroom does not meet typical standards" without attaching an emotion to her words, it may help her mother think of this situation without thinking about the shame or pain that is usually associated with the conversation.

- **Appeal**. On the other hand, maybe Marie has focused so much on her mother's behavioral problems associated with her anxiety disorder that she has not really connected emotionally with her. It could be that if Marie says, "I feel uncomfortable in this bathroom," that her mother will see the situation in a new light. We can imagine that in the past, these two have argued about whose perspective is right. As long as they have kept this conversation at a cognitive (thinking) level, they have failed to connect emotionally. Chances are that, even though Marie and her mother see the bathroom differently, they still care about each other's emotions enough to make some progress here.

- Listen. Marie has probably made numerous false assumptions about the way her mother sees the bathroom. She probably does not really understand what inhibits her mother from doing this task. Most likely, she cannot imagine the barriers that her mother feels when she considers getting it clean. It could be that if Marie listens to her mother, some missing pieces of the story will fall into place. These could complete the picture and allow her and her mother to make some progress on this issue. They may even begin to help each other get the work done.

- Sacrifice. It is also possible that if Marie decides to stop teaching, complaining, or appealing and simply starts cleaning the bathroom, that her mother will see this effort. In time, her mom may get the point. She might see that the bathroom is in need of more attention and that Marie is doing an unfair amount of the work. This quiet servitude could create enough peace in the home for her mother to reflect and, eventually, to begin helping.

- Do nothing. If Marie refuses to clean the bathroom, it is possible that, given enough time, her mother will eventually be disgusted enough to clean it herself or to help. We don't know how long it will take or if Marie can handle the stand-off, but maybe Marie can win this one if she waits it out.

- **Leave.** This option has guaranteed success for the specific outcome we are considering here. Marie will have a cleaner bathroom if she moves out. There are, of course, great costs associated with this option, both relational and financial.

- **Make a boundary.** If Marie tells her mother that she will reduce her rent payment until she gets some cooperation, her mother may help clean the bathroom. This could alert her mother to the severity of the problem or, perhaps, the cost would even be worth it to her.

- **Compromise.** If Marie and her mother reach a compromise where they each do a share of the work, then this option is successful at achieving the desired goal of a cleaner bathroom.

- **Repent.** It could be that if Marie repents of her own sin —resentment, bad attitude, etc.—her mother's heart will be softened and touched. Maybe the relationship is just waiting for one partner to "break," and then they will see great progress. Perhaps Marie just needs to be the first to take a step of humility, and her mother will follow.

WHAT IF IT DOESN'T WORK?

As I noted above, each of the nine options for relational change has potential to get Marie's mother to help clean the bathroom.

On the other hand, we cannot say with certainty that any of them will "work." But that does not mean she should choose only the option that has the greatest likelihood of achieving her mother's compliance. Even if any of these options fails to enlist her mother's help, each of these strategies still achieves a great deal of good. We can redefine the criteria of what it means for something to "work."

Let's consider some of the other positive outcomes besides getting Marie's mom to clean.

- Marie will be less frustrated. All of these options could result in this outcome. If she makes an emotional appeal, she should feel less frustrated now that her feelings are no longer bottled up. Or if she makes a simple teaching statement, she could be less frustrated now that she said what she needed to say. If she sacrifices or does nothing as an intentional act, she will be less frustrated because she will have taken control of the situation and of her own emotions. And if she leaves, she will be less frustrated now that she has the bathroom she desires.

- Marie will maintain a sense of "self." If Marie makes an emotional appeal or teaches something to her mother, her mother may be completely dismissive or become extremely angry. Either way, Marie will have maintained her right to believe and feel the way she does. She will have asserted herself in a healthy way and maintained her sense of personal dignity.

- Marie's mom will feel more loved. Listening is an act of love. We all want to be known, understood, and heard. Maybe listening doesn't get the bathroom clean, but it wasn't getting clean anyway. At least if Marie listens empathically to her mother, there will be progress in their relationship.

- Marie will be confident that she has done the right thing. If Marie reaches a compromise with her mother, it is possible that her mom will fail to live up to her side of the agreement. But Marie will at least know she has done her part in the mutual role of discipleship that they play in each other's lives. Marie will have the satisfaction of knowing that she used this opportunity to help each of them grow.

- Marie will become a more loving person. If Marie repents of her sin, she could be the only one who owns up to responsibility. Her mother may not return the favor; she may be too blind to even see her faults. But Marie will be right with God, and she will have acted lovingly toward her mother.

- Marie's mom will know the truth about the situation. It's hard to imagine if Marie teaches her mom about the bathroom's actual condition, that a "light bulb" will come on in her mom's head, and she will immediately start to help. But over time, the truth is likely to sink in, especially if it is not clouded with negative emotion, sarcasm, or ridicule. The truth is liberating, and there is something liberating about speaking it aloud.

- Marie and her mother could have a stronger emotional connection three years from now. If Marie makes an emotional appeal to her mother, it may not cause her mom to immediately change her ways. But over time, her mother will know her better. She will become accustomed to hearing what it sounds like for someone to make an emotional appeal. She will have an example of expressing emotions that could help her learn to do the same.

- Marie's mother will experience the grace of Christ in her daughter. If Marie sacrifices by making the intentional decision to serve her mother, then her mom will be the recipient of Christ's grace, and Marie will have the joy of being used by God in this way.

The initial goal of getting her mother to clean the bathroom is not the only positive outcome in this situation. Having listed several others, it is also clearly not the most noble or worthy outcome that Marie should be trying to achieve. The desired outcome, therefore, must be carefully considered before evaluating which of the nine options to pursue.

If Marie's desired outcome is her mother's cooperation, then she will choose the option above that has the greatest potential for getting her help. But there are other reasons for choosing to follow a course of action that may not produce the results one was initially hoping for.

Marie wants a clean bathroom, but she also wants less frustration. She wants to be a more loving person, and she wants her mother to feel loved by her. She wants to maintain her sense of "self."

Now we find ourselves with too many good choices! It raises the question:

HOW DO YOU CHOOSE WHICH OPTION FOR RELATIONAL CHANGE?

In a sense, this is an impossible question to answer. I can't say which of these nine positive options for relational change Marie should start with or which she should end with. I do not list them in this book in a hierarchical order. I do not suggest that one should simply go clockwise around the chart, nor do I suggest that you pick from the options that will get the other person to change their behavior. I say this for three reasons.

First, getting someone else to change their behavior is very difficult. I would not bother writing a book on changing other people's behavior because it is too big of a task with too little assurance of success. I think it's more realistic to aim for the results that are within my control, rather than the control of another person. I would rather put my eggs in the basket that I am carrying than in someone else's basket.

Secondly, it is too difficult to predict which positive option will be most effective at changing someone else's behavior. You don't know if the other person will "break" as soon as you connect with them emotionally or teach them some simple truth. Or if you are the first person to repent, you don't know if they will be touched by your Christ-like example of sacrifice.

Thirdly, and most importantly, getting someone else to change their behavior is shortsighted and aims too low. At times, I may succeed at getting compliance from people and still fail to make them feel loved. I can get a change in behavior without understanding them, speaking truth to them, being a Christ-like example to them, maintaining my sense of self, or connecting with them emotionally. But certainly, we want to achieve all of these things in our relationships!

Now I've said I don't have a particular order and that I've excluded "getting a change in behavior" as a noble goal, but that does not mean I don't have a clear criterion for choosing which option is best for relational change. I have a strong bias about how to choose. I believe this criterion will help us achieve all of the desired outcomes. The criterion can be put like this:

WHAT IS IN THE BEST INTEREST OF THE OTHER PERSON?

I recommend an others-centered approach. This approach is biblical. Paul said, "Do nothing out of selfish ambition or vain conceit. Rather, in humility value others above yourselves, not looking to your own interests but each of you to the interests of the others" (Phil. 2:3-4). In other words, the Bible recommends an alternative criterion for choosing how to act.

Most people act with the purpose of changing another person's behavior. But the Bible calls us to act in the best interest of the other person! When faced with multiple ways to respond to another person's words or deeds, we want to ask, "What's my first instinct? What's my right? What will change their behavior?" Instead, we should ask:

"HOW WOULD GOD HAVE ME ACT IN THIS SITUATION?"

This is unquestionably a better criterion. But in the following chapters, I will plough ahead with the other-centered approach. One reason is that I think the answers to both questions are identical. God would have us act in the best interest of others. Another reason is that we should ask what God should have us do in all situations, not just relational ones. But this book is primarily about horizontal relationships, so the others-centered criterion is a particular development of the God-centered question. By asking, "What is in the best interest of the other person," we have a practical way to answer the more general question, "What would God have me do?"

NOT STRATEGIES, BUT GOOD THINGS

To some extent, the nine options for relational change that I provide in this book are strategies. If you listen to your husband or wife better, it is likely to pay off. If you compromise with coworkers, you are likely to get some of the things you are asking for in return. And if you make effective emotional appeals to your friends, you are likely to connect with them and have some payoff in return.

But thinking of these options as strategies is neither noble nor wise. It is not noble because your actions are essentially strategic, so your motive is manipulative. It is not wise because there are no guarantees how others will respond. Listening is not a strategy; it is a good thing. It makes people feel loved. Making an emotional appeal is not a strategy; it is a good thing. It helps people connect and grow. Teaching is not a strategy; it is a good thing. It is a ministry to another person.

In other words, I am not arguing that there is usually only one right option for relational change. Instead, my hope is to illustrate that you are never out of options. You are not trapped.

DO PEOPLE CHANGE?

I have often heard, "People can't change." And I have a fair bit of personal experience that reinforces that thought. However, I would not have embarked on a Ph.D. in pastoral counseling if I thought people couldn't change.

Before making a commitment to that course of study, I spoke with many counselors and psychologists who assured me that people can, and sometimes do, change. People do not change the core traits of their personality. They don't go from being introverted to extroverted or serious to funny. But people do learn and practice behavioral changes.

This book is about options for relational change. It is important to note here that the book is not about changing other people. It's about changing relationships. You can change a relationship by changing your behavior. A change in relationship does not require the other person changing . . . it starts with you!

Back to Marie's story. She came to me asking, "How do I get my mom to stop hoarding?" I cannot answer that question. But I can offer nine things Marie can do to change her relationship with her mother. These suggestions may result in a change in her mother's behavior. But even if her mom keeps hoarding, Marie can create a healthier relationship.

OUT OF THE TRAP

Marie told me that she was encouraged by our conversation. When she first presented to me the situation with her mother and the bathroom, she said she felt trapped. She believed that she had exhausted every option and that nothing else was going to work.

We brainstormed several options, each of which had some potential to achieve the result she was looking for. And all of them could produce positive results, even though these results were not the sorts of changes she had originally been looking for.

You may feel trapped as well. But you have options. Let's explore the nine positive options for relational change and learn how to practice them in your relationships.

Figure 1: Nine options for relational change

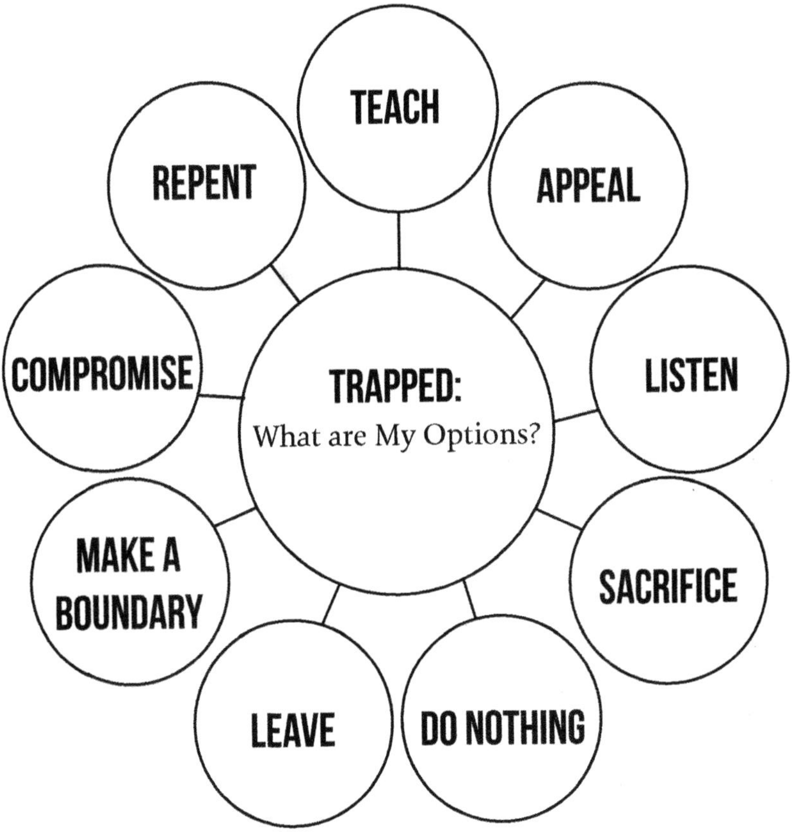

TEACH

REPENT

APPEAL

COMPROMISE

LISTEN

TRAPPED:
What are My Options?

MAKE A
BOUNDARY

SACRIFICE

LEAVE

DO NOTHING

Figure 1: Nine options for relational change.

CHAPTER 1

TEACH

ONE WAY MARIE CAN HANDLE this situation is to simply teach her mother the truth about the bathroom. She could explain that the bathroom is less hygienic than one would find in a typical home. Then she could clean it and tell her mom that this is what a clean bathroom looks like. It would be naïve to think that after making her declaration that the bathroom is disgusting, her mother would have an epiphany and decide to live a cleaner lifestyle. But if Marie sows this thought without judgment or anger, perhaps repugnance of the situation will seep in and slowly begin to churn in her mother's mind. Marie may say, "I've already tried talking to her about the situation." But has she?

More than likely, she has accompanied the simple truth with her own emotions and judgments. The truth probably came out sprinkled with sarcasm, ridicule, anger, and frustration. It could be that a statement of simple truth is all her mother needs in order to reflect on the *situation*, without the distraction of an emotional reaction from her daughter (anger, frustration) or herself (shame, guilt, exhaustion).

Even if the payoff of the statement is not immediate, Marie has accomplished several things by this simple, straightforward strategy of teaching for relational change.

- She has maintained her own voice. Marie has a right to believe the bathroom is unacceptable, and she has a right for her thoughts to be heard.

- She has mitigated her own anger. By taking steps now to resolve the situation, she has prevented herself from "blowing up" later. If she believes there is nothing she can do today, her current resentment will likely turn into future rage.

- She has fulfilled her role as a mutual discipler in her mother's life. Proverbs 27:17 says, "As iron sharpens iron, so one person sharpens another." In other words, we help make each other better, more holy, as we relate to our friends and family. Marie's mother has a rightful place in her life to be that "sharpening iron." Marie also has that role in the lives of her close friends and family. When she tells the truth about the bathroom, she plays a role in her family's discipleship.

DEFINITION OF "TEACH"

"A non-emotional explanation of the truth and consequences."

This definition is carefully written with several important words. I suggest four guidelines here:

- The statement is non-emotional.
- There is no demand for a response.

- You simply tell the truth about the situation, and if applicable, the consequences.
- If applicable, you can offer repentance.

My wife practices this type of relational teaching in her classroom as a second grade teacher. Naturally, her priorities for teaching are the basics, like English and math. But lessons about courtesy and ethics arise from time to time as well.

Recently, one of her students complained to her, "Jose called me a freak." As a teacher with 30 students in the class, and several other priorities to consider, she certainly doesn't have the time to launch an investigation as to whether this is true or why it happened. Even if she did have the time, she does not have the desire to argue with second graders, which is the inevitable result. And even if she had the desire, she does not have the ability to force the second graders in her classroom to tell her the truth. Similar to the main reason she is in the classroom, her options are quite limited in this case to "teaching."

My wife is savvy, and she knew the most expedient and effective way to deal with this was to say to Jose, "I'm not going to argue with you. I'm just going to teach you. It is not nice to call other people names, like 'freak.' In this classroom, we say only encouraging things to each other."

Predictably, Jose said, "But I didn't . . . " To which my wife stopped him short and replied, "I didn't say whether you called Brian any names. I'm reminding you that it is rude to call people names."

Jose tried a second time to argue his innocence, and my wife gave a response similar to her first one—teaching, rather than investigating. Then Jose got the point. This is not an argument or an investigation. This is a learning opportunity, and Teacher is going to get the last word.

In many of our relationships, we hope for more influence, vulnerability, investment, and time than school teachers have in their relationship with their children. So this interchange would be unsatisfying for most of us if it characterized our typical approach to conflict or communication.

But the "teaching" approach has many advantages. It does not try to accomplish outcomes outside of its control; it avoids argument; and it communicates truth. It is not adversarial, but neither is it passive. Most importantly, this approach releases one from the hope of convincing other people to change their mind. The burden of the "power of persuasion" doesn't rest with you. It resides, instead, in the simple truth behind your short message, which lingers on in the other person's mind and heart long after you have stopped talking.

Another reason that teaching is a good strategy for relational change is that truth is self-authenticating. Eventually, truth proves itself. Truth continues to confront the false beliefs that we hold, and we wonder why things don't make sense. Then we realize we have been shaking our fist at truth, but the fight against it is frustrating. We give in, end our struggle, and are relieved when we finally accept the truth because at last the world makes sense.

For example, if I were living in Antarctica, I could try to convince myself and others that it is actually warm. I could defy my friends' protests and take off layers of clothing to show how strongly I hold this conviction. But despite my efforts to convince myself and my friends that I'm warm, there will be this nagging voice in my head that says, "But it is cold." That voice doesn't need to come from my friends, or scientists, or even a thermometer. The facts will speak for themselves and will act upon me. I will be cold because it is cold, not because someone proved it to me.

It is liberating to realize how the self-authenticating nature of truth applies to relationships. I counseled a young man for about a year, and I was certain on the first day that I met him that he had a problem with alcoholism.

I knew that convincing someone they have a drinking problem is about one of the hardest cases that anyone can win. So I trusted that the facts would speak for themselves.

I told him that people who are addicted to alcohol have certain problems, and I listed a few. They can't keep their jobs; their marriages often fall apart; they have friends or family members who complain about their drinking; they can't have fun without drinking, etc.

Over the next few months, his life imploded in many of the ways that I described. Unfortunately, drinking is so addictive that many people struggle for the rest of their lives. But in this man's case, the facts were self-authenticating. I never needed to *prove* to him that he had a drinking problem because the wreck of his life did that without me. By speaking the truth, which simply echoed the circumstantial evidence he was already seeing, I helped foster relational change.

As we speak truth, we have two things on our side—the self-authenticating nature of truth and the Holy Spirit. With this in mind, we can define our own role modestly. We need not continue striving with people, taking every argument to some point of completion, whether exhaustion or agreement. We can plant the seed, and let it do its job.

My wife and I also used truth to foster change in our relationship with one of our sons. There was a period when my son would lie to us. Often, I would say something like, "I believe you are lying. If you continue to lie, you will harden your heart. You need to repent and confess in order to make your relationship right with us and with God."

Beyond that, there were many other things I was tempted to accomplish. What I really wanted was for him to agree that he lied and to tell the truth. But at times, it is nearly impossible to convince someone of something.

So I remember on one occasion, I prayed, "God, how do I convince him that he is lying?" The clear answer I heard from God is, "You can't. And besides, I've already done that."

Jesus said of the Holy Spirit, "When He comes, He will prove the world to be in the wrong about sin and righteousness and judgment" (John 16:8). As I was trying to convince my son, God revealed to me that I was outside of my jurisdiction. My job is to teach. God's job is to perfect (sanctify).

Paul said that we are temples of the Holy Spirit and that the Spirit dwells within us. Now, how do I compete with that? Even if I got an inch away from my son's face and said, "You're lying," God would still be closer, in his soul, speaking even stronger to him. And even if I yelled loudly, God's voice would be even louder.

The book of Hebrews says that "the Word of God is alive and active. Sharper than any double-edged sword, it penetrates even to dividing soul and spirit, joints and marrow; it judges the thoughts and attitudes of the heart" (Heb. 4:12). God made it clear to me that He is more invested in my son's heart than I am. I was enlisted by God to help Him accomplish His task of discipling my son. I am merely an additional voice, echoing the already present and sufficiently-powerful voice of the Holy Spirit living within him.

That day, I resigned from my futile task of demanding results and took on the much more reasonable task of supplementing and confirming God's Word. And God confirmed for me that this was the right choice because the next morning something unprecedented happened.

Without being asked or prompted in any way, my son came up to me and said, "I'm sorry, Dad. I lied." This was one of the moments in my life where I was physically brought to my knees and overcome by the profound sense of awe and worship. God can easily do what I have tried to do all of my years as a parent. He alone can soften the heart.

Finding contentment in speaking a word of truth is an act of faith. If your coworker has a bad attitude, and you simply spoke the truth, "You could have a more positive attitude," you could now rest your case. You can do so because you are convinced that the truth will do its job. It will churn. It will grow. It will do the nagging for you.

In fact, continuing to harp on the point we want to make demonstrates a lack of faith in God's ability to do as He says. Isaiah wrote,

> As the rain and the snow come down from heaven, and do not return to it without watering the earth and making it bud and flourish, so that it yields seed for the sower and bread for the eater, so is my Word that goes out from my mouth: It will not return to me empty, but will accomplish what I desire and achieve the purpose for which I sent it" (Isa. 55:10-11).

If you believe that God's Word will accomplish His purpose, then your role is actually quite small. You are one of many voices of truth.

You have the ability to create relational change in contexts all around you by teaching truths. There is a gracious, non-demanding, non-emotional way to communicate truth. It can be so effective that the truth speaks for itself. Here are three examples:

- Shelly's teenage son was getting into the car with his siblings, and he noticed he was about to be last in the car. Realizing he was about to lose the front passenger seat, he yelled out, "Shotgun," and pushed his little brother out of the way, managing to get in his preferred seat. His mom said directly to him, "That wasn't very nice, was it?" She taught the truth. This self-controlled statement helped foster change because the words sank in and percolated over time.

- The accountant at Seth's office has a habit of sending terse emails. Nearly all of Seth's coworkers have commented how these emails rub them the wrong way. But everyone is afraid to talk to the accountant about it because in the past she has become extremely angry when confronted. Seth replied to her latest rude email by simply telling the accountant, "This email strikes me as an accusation." He non-emotionally spoke the truth about the situation, without demanding a response.

- Ron has an employee who had a run-in with a client. The employee decided to handle the situation in a certain way without consulting anyone else in the company. Ron approached the employee and simply said, "That's not the procedure we are following." Then Ron briefly explained the preferred procedure.

In each of these situations, the speaker offered a non-emotional explanation about the truth of the situation. None of the speakers demanded an immediate response.

SPEAKING THE TRUTH FOR RELATIONAL CHANGE

A frustrated friend of mine named John asked, "Why am I the only person who apologizes? How come no one in my world apologizes to me?" Before I answer a question, I like to explore all possible choices, even the outlandish ones, just so I can be sure I have fully considered the issue.

So I answered, "As far as I can tell, there are three reasons why people would not apologize to you. First, it could be that no one is sinning against you. That is very unlikely. Secondly, it could be that people are apologizing, and you are not noticing or hearing it. That's worth considering. Thirdly, it could be that the reason you apologize to others is that they confront you, ask you to apologize, or tell you that they are upset. Maybe you are not asking anyone to apologize."

The notion that John should ask others to apologize was difficult for him to swallow. His resistance to the idea was partly a result of the fact that the model supplied by those around him was unhealthy. People didn't really "ask" him for an apology; they demanded, accused, or confronted. But it is possible to solicit an apology without being angry or overly confrontational.

Let's assume John's good friend was very late coming to his house, and, consequently, they arrived at the movies halfway through the film. Most likely, the friend feels at least a little self-conscious about being late, and, if John confronts him while on the way to the movies, he will be defensive. But the next day, John can call his friend (or say face to face), "I would appreciate an apology for your being late to my house yesterday."

This is the most basic form of relational teaching—simple, clear, honest, and humble. It is simple because John is speaking only of one specific action which occurred yesterday. It is clear, especially since John is making a specific request of what he would like. It is honest because John neither bottles up his emotions nor overstates the situation. And it is humble because John is not making himself better than his friend by calling him names or making sweeping accusations.

When children approach adulthood, it is vital that parents favor teaching over the other options in this book, especially for discipline. Tim had a rule that his children not wear both earbuds while around other people. When his son reached the age of 18, he would occasionally violate this rule. Tim was reluctant to simply say to his adult son, "Take your earbuds out." So Tim explained the truth and consequences of this behavior. He said, "Wearing your earbuds around other people isolates you from them. It is also considered rude." He simply told the truth (it is rude) and stated the consequences (it isolates people).

These strategies of truth-teaching do not involve an emotional appeal. An emotional appeal would not be wrong, but it wouldn't be teaching for relational change. By saying, "Wearing earbuds around other people isolates you from them," Tim is not demanding a response. He is not asking for agreement, an apology, or even for his son to take out the earbuds. He is teaching the truth to his son, so that it can penetrate his son's heart all on its own. Truth can work on its own.

There are several reasons that I say parents should favor teaching as their children get older. The first is practical. As your kids get older, your influence upon them changes and your options for gaining compliance from them diminish. As a matter of shrewd strategy, you should not put yourself in a position of asking for things you cannot control, demand, or enforce. This would be frustrating since your demands could go unmet, and it also undermines your authority because your kids will get the message that you cannot enforce the things you ask. Also, it hardens their heart because you teach them that they can disobey without consequences.

Another reason I teach parents to favor teaching as a strategy for relational change with their children is that teaching prepares children for life. For example, Tim's goal is not to have a child who refrains from wearing earbuds. His goal is to have a child who is well-connected to others, has an inviting demeanor, is considerate of others, etc.

THE NEGATIVE COUSINS TO TEACHING: SARCASM, RIDICULE, INTERROGATION, CONVINCEMENT

As I have pastored and engaged in personal counseling sessions, I have coached many people in the skills found in this book. One observation I have made in coaching people on the skill of "teaching" is that nearly everyone believes they are teaching when they are not. Many people are convinced that they are good communicators and that they say things in a straightforward manner. But we are not as great at communication as we like to think. We often employ negative cousins to teaching—such as sarcasm, ridicule, interrogation, argument, or subtle hinting.

I learned about unclear teaching as a teenager. My first job was at a grocery store as an assistant meat cutter. During my first week, the manager said to me, "Dan, if you have any questions, let me know."

"Thanks," I replied.

"Any questions at all, don't hesitate to ask," he reiterated.

I assured him, "I will."

"So, do you have any questions?" he pressed.

"Not right now."

"Well, last night, you cut a whole sirloin the wrong direction, and now it's ruined."

I obviously had no idea that I had ruined the sirloin, but it was less obvious to the manager that I had no idea why he wondered if I had any questions.

Maybe you're thinking that I should have picked up on the clues. If I had been older, I might have. But nevertheless, we all fail to pick up on the clues around us. We often need the truth spelled out in simple, clear terms.

It is condescending to try to convince someone else. It implies that the other person's opinion is not valid or that they would see it your way if they had all the information. Think of your political opinions. You have probably given a lifetime of thought to some political issues, and you have shaped, modified, and refined your convictions through reflection and education.

Now imagine a friend of yours catches wind that you have an opposite view to hers, so she says to you, "I'd really like to sit down with you and have a conversation about this, to tell you why I think you're wrong." Doesn't sound very inviting, does it?

None of us is as good at communicating as we think we are, and none of us understands the people around us as much as we think we do. I have known my wife for over 20 years, and I just recently learned that I had been misinterpreting an oft-quoted statement of hers.

Occasionally, she begins a sentence with, "It would have been nice . . . " My son recently let my wife borrow his car. When she left in the morning, she noticed that it was out of gas, but she had not prepared enough time to fill up, so she was late for work.

That night, she said to our son, "It would have been nice if I had known that there was no gas." I interpreted this statement as "shame on you for not telling me" or "I'm mad at you for not telling me." So I asked my wife what she wants when she says the phrase, "It would have been nice." She explained, "So next time, if you think of it, could you let me know?"

Honestly, even after 20 years, I did not know that was the implied information in her sentence about "what would have been nice." I thought it was meant to evoke guilt and shame, but she was actually making a simple request. It may have seemed straightforward to you, and it certainly seemed straightforward to her, but we can all be blinded by conflict. We are blinded by defensiveness or fear.

Another negative cousin of *teaching* is shaming. Sometimes this can take the form of accusatory questions. Let's imagine, for instance, that a father observes his daughter grab a toy forcefully from her sister. The father might ask, "How would you feel if she did that to you?" The question has some value, but it is not as effective as we might think.

First, it assumes that the listener has enough capacity for self-reflection, which is surprisingly limited in some people, especially when they are on the defensive.

Second, the question does not explicitly communicate the truth behind it.

Third, the question sets up the accused to give a sarcastic answer. It's better to just say, "It was unkind to take that toy." Unless I thought I was begging for an argument, I might answer the question for my daughter by teaching her how she would feel—"You would feel angry if your sister did that to you." I also might add, "You feel guilty for being selfish, and I'm sure she will forgive you if you ask."

HOW TO TEACH FOR RELATIONAL CHANGE

The key to effective teaching for relational change is to keep it short. You don't want your emotion to cloud the truth, nor do you want your verbosity to cause exhaustion. The value of brevity is attested from several angles. An economic principle, philosophical principle, and theological principle support the idea that shorter is better.

In Economics, there is the "Law of Diminishing Returns." This principle essentially states that you get "less bang for your buck" as time goes on. You get a high return for the initial investment of energy; but as time goes on, the more energy you expend, the less payoff you get for each additional increment.

I spoke earlier of the "self-authenticating nature of truth." This principle basically states that truth does not need your help. In fact, the greater effort required to convince someone indicates a problem, since truth should have been able to prove itself. If you speak the truth to someone, even if they are defiant or uninterested, you can have confidence that it will sink into their heart and resonate with what their soul already knows to be true.

Theologically, we know from Isaiah 55:11 that God's Word does not return void but accomplishes what He sets it out to do. Jesus said that the role of the Holy Spirit is to convict the world of sin, righteousness, and judgment. This means that the Holy Spirit is able to do a better job than you can of convincing others of the truth.

Keeping your teaching short is an act of faith. It demonstrates that you believe the Holy Spirit exists, is active, and is effective. You are sowing a seed and turning the job over to the Holy Spirit to do the rest to make the seed take root and grow.

Even if we become experts at teaching others with clear, simple, loving truth, this may not always be the best response. Going back to the criterion that guides us (what is best for the other person), we may reconsider whether or not to teach.

My wife and I discovered once that teaching for relational change was not the right option with our son. He was late on his first day to work at a new job. When he came home that evening, we asked him how the day went. He was visibly disturbed by the fact that he was 15 minutes late. My wife delivered a simple, clear teaching: "That was irresponsible." She abided by the guidelines listed here for teaching. But judging by our son's reaction, it was obvious that he already knew he was irresponsible and that he was grieving. So even the best delivery of teaching may not be what the other person needs to hear.

WHAT INCREASES YOUR CHANCES OF SUCCESS?

What target are you aiming for? Before we open our mouths, it is helpful to strategize by asking what bull's eye we are trying to hit. One time I asked a frustrated mom who I was counseling, "What was your goal when you were talking to your son?" She said, "I never thought about that. I was just really mad."

Sometimes our goal is to let off steam. Often the goal is to get compliance from another person. Sometimes we want agreement or an apology. When teaching for relational change, we aim for a more realistic and modest goal. But the goal also happens to be the most valuable—to supplement or echo God's voice in communicating the truth.

In Ephesians 4:15, Paul exhorts us to "speak the truth in love." David Augsburger refers to the concept of "speaking the truth in love" as *truthing*. He offers this definition: "When I speak, I want to speak simply—to say what I mean in the clearest, shortest, frankest words I know. I want to speak personally. I want to speak for myself, not for others. I will try not to speak for you. I want to speak honestly. I want to speak directly."[1]

Though the title of this chapter is "Teach," there is a risk in teaching that we come across as condescending. Perhaps "truthing" is a better option because it does not imply that you are in a mightier position or that you know more than the other person. Sometimes it may be your role to teach, but often, in relationships, you were not assigned the task. It is, however, always your role to "speak the truth in love." Augsburger gives these tips for doing it:

> Truthing is the word we have been using in this chapter to designate simplicity, clarity, honesty, and humility in communication. Truthing seeks simplicity in its preference for single-level statements and open-ended questions. Truth seeks clarity in its intention to not seduce, coerce,

---

1 Augsburger, *Caring Enough to Confront*, 30-31.

dominate, or control. Truthing strives for honesty—not the so-called honesty of radical openness that ventilates without considering the impact on the receiver, but the honesty of thoughtful integrity and centered trustworthiness. Truthing prizes humility, recognizing that we know in part, see in part, and understand in part. Truthing finds its core meaning in the two shortest and most powerful words (yes and no)—saying a genuine yes to the other, yes to life together in relationship, yes to moral integrity in what we are and do; speaking no to what diminishes self or other, no to what destroys relationship, no to what falls short of moral integrity.[2]

Teaching has great power to cause relational change because you are not depending on the power of your persuasion, emotion, or perseverance. The power behind your words is the truth itself.

IS IT EVER OK TO SHOW EMOTION WHEN TEACHING FOR RELATIONAL CHANGE?

I explained the concept of "truthing" to Trisha during one of our counseling sessions. When she heard that "truthing" is a non-emotional explanation of the truth and the consequences, she said, "Is it ever OK to show emotion?" Well, of course you can show emotion whenever you see fit, but realize that doing so often comes at a cost. That doesn't mean you should never do it; it just means that showing emotion may be at cross-purposes with letting the simple truth percolate in the other person's mind. The more emotional your appeal is, the less you will be practicing the skills in this chapter (but you will be practicing the skills in another chapter).

---

2 Augsburger, *Caring Enough to Confront*, 37.

So the question is not what you are allowed to do, but rather which of the nine options for change you think is best with this person, at this moment. In other words, the question is not, "Am I allowed to show emotion?" but "Is an expression of emotion going to be effective at reaching my current goal?"

Emotional appeals can be very effective, and that's why the next chapter is devoted to those skills. But an emotional appeal has a different effect than "truthing." If you are considering what is going to be more effective, you need to first ask what you want to accomplish.

An emotional appeal can accomplish the following:

- Connection (let the other person understand and know you better),
- A catharsis (possibly make you feel better since you "vented"),
- Fear (make the other person afraid to cross you in the future), or
- Proof (the other person will see just how mad you actually are).

"Truthing," on the other hand, has different effects:

- Plants a seed (It allows the truth to work in their heart),
- Ensures relational stability (Since you are not asking for a response, the conflict ends for the time being.),
- Fosters connection with the Holy Spirit (You confirm what the Spirit has already told them.)

WHAT TEACHING LOOKS LIKE IN THE BIBLE

Jesus practiced the type of truthing described in this chapter. He said, "You have heard that it was said, 'You shall not commit adultery.'

But I tell you that anyone who looks at a woman lustfully has already committed adultery with her in his heart" (Matt. 5:27-28).

Jesus expressed deep emotion on several occasions. He wept at the death of Lazarus and at the sight of Jerusalem and was moved with compassion when He saw the crowds. But in this case, the appeal is non-emotional. There is no demand for a response. He is not asking anyone to agree, disagree, or respond. He merely states the truth about the situation—lust constitutes adultery. The consequences are implied, but understood by His audience. People who commit adultery break the sixth commandment and must repent or risk becoming covenant-breakers. This is the non-emotional truth, without a demand for response.

When Jesus was questioned about whether it was lawful to pay taxes to Caesar, Jesus answered, "Then give back to Caesar what is Caesar's, and to God what is God's" (Lk. 20:25). Similarly, adversaries asked Jesus why divorce was allowed in the Bible if it did not fit into God's plan. Jesus replied, "Moses permitted you to divorce your wives because your hearts were hard. But it was not this way from the beginning" (Matt. 19:8). In these instances, Jesus gave simple instructions. He simply taught the truth about the situation. There were no emotional pleas or requirement of a response.

Here are a couple other examples from Jesus:

- He said, "Again I tell you, it is easier for a camel to go through the eye of a needle than for someone who is rich to enter the kingdom of God" (Matt. 19:24). In this aphorism, Jesus non-emotionally states the truth about the situation—it is difficult for the rich to go to heaven. He implicitly communicates the consequences—loving/

hoarding wealth will result in damnation. He does not demand a response from any of His hearers, but instead simply offers the truth to those who will listen.

- Jesus said, "I am the light of the world. Whoever follows me will not walk in darkness, but will have the light of life" (Jn. 8:12). To this, the Pharisees said, "Here you are, appearing as your own witness; your testimony is not valid" (Jn. 8:13). How would you have responded to them? Many of us would be offended, angry, defensive, argumentative, or dismissive. Jesus simply taught—consistent with the definition I've given in this chapter—non-emotionally stating the truth and consequences. He said, "If you knew me, you would know my Father also" (Jn. 8:19b).

Pastor Tom Holladay picks up on Jesus' strategy in *The Relationship Principles of Jesus*. In offering tips to troubleshoot communication, Holladay suggests we "give a clear, confident response instead of reacting defensively."[3] This is often how Jesus responded when He was confronted.

John the Baptist had a clear message of truth for those who went into the desert to see him. He said, "Repent, for the kingdom of heaven has come near" (Matt. 3:2). John's message stated the truth about the situation, without appealing to emotion. John was not demanding a response (which would have been out of his control); instead, he was answering the question, "What should we do then?" (Lk. 3:10).

King David's adultery with Bathsheba resulted in pregnancy. Out of fear that the adultery would be exposed, David conceived a

---

3 Holladay, *The Relationship Principles of Jesus*, 184.

cover-up. He ordered Bathsheba's husband, who was a soldier named Uriah, to be placed at the front of the battle lines and then for the troops to back away from him. This would result in Uriah's death and make it possible for David to marry Bathsheba.

The prophet Nathan knew what occurred, and he confronted David. The biting words are recorded for us, "You are the man" (2 Sam. 12:7). Nathan's "truthing" exhibited the characteristics I suggest in this chapter. Nathan's words were non-emotional, and he did not demand a response or apology—the consequences of David's actions were already obvious. He simply stated the truth about the situation.

Since Moses led over a million Israelites out of Egypt, he was quickly overwhelmed with his administrative duties. Moses took on all three branches of government. He was the chief executive, lawgiver, and judge. His father-in-law, Jethro, knew this was inefficient, unhealthy, and impossible. Jethro said simply to Moses, "What you are doing is not good" (Exod. 18:17). He followed that statement with practical suggestions for how to delegate the responsibilities. But Jethro's words were non-emotional and did not demand a response. Jethro told the truth about the situation (again, the consequences were obvious).

WHAT TEACHING LOOKS LIKE IN MARRIAGE

Keith's wife is often late, and this causes tension in their relationship. He says he does not want or expect to change his wife, Jen. He's heard often enough the advice that you don't go into marriage trying to change someone. But because he makes comments from time to time about her being late, she can tell that he really does see her tardiness as a character flaw.

He has employed various strategies to communicate his irritation with her being late. He tried to set her clock fast, set the alarm on her cell phone, write notes, etc. He would make comments like, "I'm going to be on time, how about you?" And he would drive separate cars to the same destination, just to make sure that he wouldn't be late.

The persistent tardiness after 20 years of marriage dumbfounds him, in light of how often he has communicated irritation and despite all of his creative attempts. He has addressed her late arrivals in all forms of language—sarcastic, subtle, direct, humorous, etc. Yet still no change. Clearly, Jen's tardiness will not be solved by better education or communication.

What Keith doesn't realize is that Jen has subconsciously figured out that Keith is not only irritated with her being late but that he has some contempt for her. She didn't ask him to set the alarm, speed up the watch, or write the notes. She has never, in fact, asked for his help in getting her somewhere on time. She does not value prompt arrivals. She is actually quite comfortable with her lifestyle, and she usually arrives at places at the time that she had hoped to. But to tell this to Keith would exacerbate the contempt that she already knows he has. She lets him believe that she is trying harder, so she doesn't have to deal with the contempt.

At the core of Keith and Jen's issue is confusion over their purpose in marriage. Their marriage is on the verge of a life-changing transformation if they could answer these questions:

- "How will I be used in the life of my spouse?"
- "What is the purpose of this relationship?"
- "Why does God have me in this marriage?"

Keith and Jen were unclear about their role in each other's lives, so they let certain assumptions about that purpose develop implicitly over time. To some extent, Keith came to see his role as parental. In other words, he implicitly believed that his role was to help Jen make better decisions and to develop mature character traits.

Perhaps it wasn't out of line for Keith to take on this teaching role in this case. Marriage has an instructive purpose. Paul wrote, "For the unbelieving husband has been sanctified through his wife, and the unbelieving wife has been sanctified through her believing husband" (1 Cor. 7:14a). Marriage is a place of instruction. The relationship needs to be one of mutual growth, and we should avoid having a parental role in marriage. But as Gary Thomas asks in *Sacred Marriage*, "What if God designed marriage to make us holy more than make us happy?"[4]

All of the options for relational change apply to marriage, but teaching has a unique role because marriage is a divine tool for our sanctification. Thomas explains, "Marriage can be the gym in which our capacity to experience and express God's love is strengthened and further developed."[5] In other words, no one is going to challenge you to grow more than your spouse. Your husband or wife will become an expert in identifying and pointing out your sin. No doubt, he or she will also offer a plan of action to change as well!

It may seem threatening, unsafe, or just plain exhausting to have a marriage partner take on the role of discipling you. But this truth can also be accepted with excitement and eager anticipation to see how God will shape you through the people around you. Thomas

---

4 Thomas, *Sacred Marriage*, 18.
5 Thomas, *Sacred Marriage*, 40.

puts it this way: "The young man in the monastery entered celibacy consciously as a path toward holiness. Is it possible to enter marriage consciously as a path toward holiness?"[6]

Not only is it possible, it is impossible to imagine that marriage will not offer an excellent forum for you to deal with your sin and to repent. "What marriage has done for me is hold up a mirror to my sin," Thomas writes. "It forces me to face myself honestly and consider my character flaws, selfishness, and anti–Christian attitudes, encouraging me to be sanctified and cleansed and to grow in godliness."[7]

From my counseling, I have discovered that people will supply various answers—even somewhat biblical answers—to the question, "What is the purpose of marriage?" Glancing at the account of Adam and Eve, some assume that the husband's role is to provide financially. (God told Adam that he would work the ground and by his sweat it would produce, according to Genesis 3:19.) Likewise, some assume that the wife's role is to bear children. (God told Eve that she would have pain in childbirth.)

The answer might seem satisfactory, since, after all, it appears so early in the history of humankind and in the Bible (Gen. 3:16-19). But even this early passage of Scripture does not supply the answer to what is the husband's and wife's role in the other person's life.

The answer is found even earlier, in Genesis 1:27, "So God created mankind in his own image, in the image of God he created them; male and female he created them." The role of the husband is to be

---

the image of God to his wife. The role of the wife is to be the image of God to her husband. Together, the two are the image of God.

In reference to the previous story, it is not Keith's role to parent his wife. Instead, his role is to be the image of God and to be one with his wife.

Then to answer the questions above, we might say:

- The purpose of marriage is to be the image of God to/with another person and to become "one."
- God has me in this marriage to show my spouse what God is like.
- I will be used by God to speak the truth about who God is and what God desires.

THE PURPOSE OF MARRIAGE

Because marriage can be difficult, people tend to set the bar low for their goals. I asked one man what his goal for his marriage was, and he said, "Not to have any bickering for the week."

Ironically, by setting the bar low, we will never achieve it. That's because our low goals are essentially self-serving, but marriage is designed to be an other-serving arrangement. So as long as our goals are wrong, no matter how low they may be, we will never achieve them since marriage is designed for another purpose.

In his book *The Marriage Builder*, Larry Crabb addresses the purpose of marriage. Crabb writes that the goal of marriage is to develop, "A deep experience of personal intimacy through relationship with a person of the opposite sex."[8] This goal is relentlessly other-centered.

---

8 Crabb, *The Marriage Builder*, 19.

But it is not self-deprecating. In other words, both partners have much to gain by self-sacrifice.

Crabb encourages, "Commit yourself to ministering to your spouse's needs, knowing that however he may respond can never rob you of your worth as a person."[9] The purpose of marriage, in other words, is to be used by God as an instrument of discipleship for your spouse.

Crabb writes about his relationship with his wife, "I regard it as part of my role as spiritual leader to help her do the best job she can as wife and mother."[10] The purpose of marriage is not primarily for our own happiness or satisfaction. Neither is it primarily for the happiness or satisfaction of our spouse. Well then, who's left?

Marriage fits a purpose within God's plan. The purpose of marriage is that the two partners will be vessels for use by God in His task of perfecting His children (you and your spouse).

Marriage, in this sense, is a ministry. It is ministry through intimacy (which Crabb calls "Soul Oneness"). He explains, "The key to achieving Soul Oneness is to maintain the fundamental goal of ministry to our partner's deepest needs and to keep that goal inviolate."[11]

In a successful marriage each day we must remind ourselves that we can be used by God in the life of our partner. Crabb summarizes this role:

> Husbands and wives are to regard marriage as an opportunity to minister in a unique and special way to another human being, to be used of God to bring their spouses into

---

9 Crabb, *The Marriage Builder*, 39.
10 Crabb, *The Marriage Builder*, 52.
11 Crabb, *The Marriage Builder*, 54.

a more satisfying appreciation of their worth as persons who are secure and significant in Jesus Christ.[12]

I mentioned earlier that Keith was confused about his role in his wife's life. If he is clear that his role is to reflect the image of God, how would he address his wife's tardiness? Let me offer a few suggestions of what he could say:

"Jen, I believe that other people are honored when we arrive at a place on time. So showing up on time is something I value, and I think we should get better at it. I imagine that you are less pressured to be on time because you value something, and I would like to understand it. How do you feel about being late? Is there something else that is even more important for you?"

If Keith says something like this to his wife, he has accomplished two things. First, he has reflected the image of God. He has graciously and lovingly spoken the truth about the situation. Secondly, he has expressed to his wife how much he values intimacy (knowing her), even more than being on time. He has begun a conversation that will help him know his wife better, which is the purpose of marriage (oneness).

In marriage, we can be used by God to reflect His image. We do this by speaking and acting the way that God does. God does not force us to act differently, and we are not able to force our spouse to act differently either. But God does speak the truth about our behavior, and we can speak the truth to our spouse about how we feel or what we believe. When we do that, we leave the results in God's hands, content that we have been used by Him.

---

12 Crabb, *The Marriage Builder*, 55.

WHAT TEACHING LOOKS LIKE IN PARENTING

While I was teaching a course at Biola University, we came to the topic of heaven. A student raised her hand and asked, "Will my dad get to be my dad in heaven?"

That question has haunted and blessed me ever since. It blessed me because I am inspired by this man whom I barely know. All I know is that his name is Joseph, and his daughter is crazy about him. I am inspired by his faithfulness to his daughter and her desire to have him as a father for eternity. Her question haunted me because it sets the bar frighteningly high. Would my children say that about me?

As students waited for me to answer, there must have been some who thought, "Please say no!" I don't, by the way, know the answer to that question, and I had to tell the class that I didn't have a good answer. But I do know I aspire to be like Joseph. I hope to be worthy of my children saying the same about me.

My daughter, Natasha, asked me, "Why do kids have to do what their parents say?" If I had just asked her to clean up her room, I wouldn't have found any charm in her question. But the timing of the question was sincere, so I gave it my best. I said, "God put children in families so that kids would learn what He is like. God is our Father, and we only know what that means if we have earthly fathers and mothers."

God could have designed humans so that we don't need people to teach us. Many animals are born independent. They don't need years of instruction. When Alaskan Salmon are born, they never see their mother or father. They hatch from an egg and, though surrounded by other hatchlings, are born independent. Nevertheless, they swim thousands of miles away and return to the very spot they were born to spawn or lay eggs the next year. God could have designed the universe in such a way that humans are born independent; but He didn't.

When we speak of God as a father, some people insist that this is a metaphor or anthropomorphism (a way of explaining God in human terms). In other words, we are taking an image with which we are familiar to describe something unknown. We understand the family, so we are able to apply that image as a metaphor to understand God as father.

But what if we got the metaphor backwards? **What if the earthly family is God's metaphor for explaining Himself to us?** That seems more likely, given that the Scriptures are a revelation from God and not simply our best effort at describing Him. What if God is the original or essential parent, and He designed the earthly family as a metaphor in order to describe to us what He is like?

We are supposed to know what it means for God to be the father by the object lesson of our families. Perhaps the earthly family is the imperfect metaphor for the heavenly reality. God designed us to be born as dependent children so that we would learn who He is. By seeing the mercy of our parents, we would understand His mercy. By experiencing our parents' grace to us, we would know His amazing grace. By receiving our parents' forgiveness, we would be assured that God is a perfect parent who also forgives us. And by living with our parent's severity and authority, we would understand what it means to submit to God "because He said so."

This understanding of parenting has a deep impact for how you will be used as a parent. Our role as parents is to represent Christ and to reflect the image of God. This role does not induce pride, heavy-handedness, or an "authority trip" within me. Instead, it overwhelms me with an impossible task of awesome responsibility.

By my obedient actions, my children will develop an understanding of who God is. By my representation as a father, my children will know what it means for God to be their father. They will learn this as I make teaching a central priority as a parent.

BEING USED BY GOD AS A PARENT TO TEACH FOR RELATIONAL CHANGE

As I mentioned earlier, my son once lied to me for the typical reason: to avoid getting in trouble. Eventually he told the truth, but a struggle with children over the truth is always exhausting. It is the battle of two human wills and evident of a spiritual struggle as well.

Shortly after the incident, I got on my bicycle and went for a ride. I spent some time in prayer, but my prayer was quite short because I was cut off by the Lord. I began, "Lord, it would have been easier if you didn't give me a child who lied . . ." Please understand, I wasn't asking for a different kid, nor a different life. I was just pointing out the obvious fact that it would have been easier . . . But in one of those few, yet strongly clear, moments where God speaks back, I heard Him distinctly say to me, "Easier for whom?"

The weight and significance of that reply has made a lasting, profound impact on me as a parent and also as a counselor. My plea to God implied that it would have been easier for me if my children didn't lie. But is my "easiness" really relevant for my role as a parent? Isn't it more relevant to ask, "Would it have been easier for my son?" If he had been raised in another home, would his growth into a mature follower of Christ have been more likely? Perhaps God knew which home would be the easiest place for him to grow and mature. But even that is beside the point.

God has a job to do. It is God's desire to raise my son into a Christ-like man, and He has asked me to do Him a favor by helping Him as He puts this young man on loan in my home. So the real question is, "Would it have been easier for God?" Would God's job of maturing my son have been easier if this young man were in my home or in the home of another? Since it is God's main prerogative to mature His children, and since God is all-powerful and all-knowing, I trust that He made the arrangements which would suit Him best.

My role as a parent is not to raise children who make me happy or to raise perfect children or kids who will be my lifelong friends. I realized that day on my lamenting bike ride that my role as a parent is to be used by God to carry out an important role in His task of raising His kids.

In *Parenting from the Inside Out,* Daniel Siegel and Mary Hartzell explain that in order to be an effective parent, we must make sense of our lives. We must make sense of our childhood, and we must have a narrative of who we are and what we are supposed to do. The central theme of the book is to create a self-identity that provides a foundational philosophy for who you are as a parent.

When my son lied, I was reminded of these important questions:

- "How will I be used as a parent?"
- "What is the purpose of this relationship?"
- "What is my role in the lives of my children?"

The Bible answers these questions for us. The Word of God explains that a parent's purpose is to be used by God to instruct his or her children. Moses wrote,

Hear, O Israel: The LORD our God, the LORD is one. Love the LORD your God with all your heart and with all your soul and with all your strength. These commandments that I give you today are to be on your hearts. Impress them on your children. Talk about them when you sit at home and when you walk along the road, when you lie down and when you get up. Tie them as symbols on your hands and bind them on your foreheads. Write them on the doorframes of your houses and on your gates (Deut. 6:4-9).

In *Shepherding a Child's Heart,* Tedd Tripp explains the connection of this passage from Deuteronomy to the task of parenting. He writes, "Whether waking, walking, talking, or resting, you must be involved in helping your child to understand life, himself, and his needs from a biblical perspective."[13] One central role of parents in the lives of their children is to teach. Teaching is the primary means of relational change.

Parents often get sidetracked with behavior. If your goal in discipline is to change behavior, it is easy to understand why this happens. The thing that alerts you to your child's need for correction is his behavior. Behavior irritates and thus calls attention to itself. Behavior becomes your focus. You think you have corrected when you have changed unacceptable behavior to behavior that you sanction and appreciate. "What's the problem?" You ask. The problem is this: your child's needs are far more profound than his aberrant behavior. Remember, his behavior does not just spring forth uncaused. His behavior—the things he says and does—reflect his heart. If you are really to help him, you must be concerned with the attitudes of heart that drive his behavior.[14]

---

13 Tripp, *Shepherding a Child's Heart,* 32.
14 Tripp, *Shepherding a Child's Heart,* 4.

As a parent, you are God's agent in this task of providing essential training and instruction in the Lord. This does not mean you have ultimate authority but that you are under authority. You have a task delegated by God. You and your child are in a similar position; you both need to submit to God's authority. You have differing roles but the same master. Tripp explains the way parents are used by God as vessels of instruction. He writes,

> As a parent you have authority because God calls you to be an authority in your child's life. You have the authority to act on behalf of God. As a father or mother you do not exercise rule over your jurisdiction but over God's. You act at His command. You discharge a duty that He has given. You may not try to shape the lives of your child as pleases you but as pleases Him.[15]

In other words, the role of a parent is not self-directed. Your expectations and rules are not subjective or relative. God is raising His children, perfecting and instructing them, and He has enlisted you in this task. As a parent, you are being used by God in His work of instruction.

Tripp explains how the role of a parent is delegated by God: "When you direct, correct, or discipline, you are not acting out of your own will; you are acting on behalf of God. You don't have to wonder if it is okay for you to be in charge. God has given you a duty to perform."[16]

WHAT PARENTS CANNOT DO

It is vital that parents clearly know their role, so that they also understand what their role is not. I was slow to learn some important

15 Tripp. *Shepherding a Child's Heart*, 28.
16 Tripp, *Shepherding a Child's Heart*, 30.

lessons that should have been obvious to me earlier. For instance, I learned with my fifth child that babies prefer to be put on the changing table gently, rather than plopped there. But one lesson I learned early was that I cannot control the behavior of my children.

Previously, I mentioned my frustration with one of my children lying. There are some things I can do and others that are impossible (though I would like to do them). I can tell my son that I think he is lying. I can tell him that lying is a sin and encourage him to repent. I can tell him that he will be punished in some particular way.

But I cannot *make* him tell the truth. I simply cannot force those words to come out of his mouth. And even if I could, I would not be able to change his heart so that he had a spirit of repentance and sorrow. I suppose I could make him sit in a chair until he told the truth, but children are often able to win these stand-offs. My role, therefore, is not to change the behavior of my children but to speak the truth about their behavior to them. I have not been charged by God to make sure my son never lies, but to instruct my son that lying is a sin and that God forgives our sins when we repent.

When I realized that my role is limited to the things I can do (rather than forcing my children to do things that are outside of my control), I found peace of mind in the Serenity Prayer: "God, grant me the serenity to accept the things I cannot change, courage to change the things I can, and wisdom to know the difference."

I cannot force my children to change, but I can instruct them. I pray for the wisdom from God to know the difference between how I can or cannot be used by Him. I know that I am not solely responsible for their actions, but I am responsible for speaking the truth to them about their actions. As a parent, you are used by God as a vessel of truth to your children.

Early in the school week, my daughter asked if she could go to the toy store. I explained to her that we would have to wait until Saturday when we had more time. This answer understandably disappointed her, so she made a pouty groan. I believed that "teaching" was in her best interest. In a situation like this many of us might be tempted to say one of the following:

- "Then we won't go if you don't want to go."
- "How would you feel if you wanted to do something nice for me, and I pouted?"
- "Why do you always act like that?"
- "Don't be such a baby."

We might look back and feel justified that we made our point by saying one of these things. We could call these statements "teaching." But it takes a mature, non-defensive, introspective person to decipher what the teaching is behind these statements.

No matter what age the other person is, they will likely have difficulty hearing through their own defensiveness. We are a numb-skulled—or to be more biblical, stiff-necked (Deut. 31:27)—bunch of people. We need the truth clearly spelled out. So a better response in the situation above would be one of the following:

- "The polite response right now is, 'Thank you, Dad.'"
- "Your response seems ungrateful."

As parents, we are able to teach with a non-emotional, non-demanding, simple explanation of the truth and consequences. The reason this skill for relational change is so effective is that God is working on the hearts of our children, even when we are silent. Long after you have spoken the truth, the Holy Spirit will echo the words you said to your kids.

Tedd Tripp explains, "The God-given conscience is your ally in discipline and correction. Your most powerful appeal will be those that smite the conscience. When the offended conscience is aroused, correction and discipline find their mark."[17]

This is liberating because it means that relational change in parenting is not a result of you winning a power struggle, nor does relational change depend upon your constant nagging, spying, and intervention. You can rest at ease knowing that truth is self-authenticated, and that the Holy Spirit is more active, more effective, and more concerned about speaking truth to your kids than you are.

We have a jar of coins in our kitchen where we empty our pockets. Once my son took a dollar out of that jar without asking. I told him that in the future, he needs to ask before taking money from the jar. Failure to do so, I said, would be stealing. He then wanted to debate whether that was technically stealing.

It is tempting for parents at this point to try to win the debate and hear those satisfying words, "OK, Dad, I agree that it was stealing. You're right." But it is not within my power to make my son believe something, nor to say something. This is not the task with which God has charged me. My role is to teach the truth as I echo the voice of the Holy Spirit, which is already at work within him convicting him of sin.

So I said to him, "That is considered stealing, and it is a sin." At this point, I am not going to keep arguing the point until he agrees

17 Tripp, *Shepherding a Child's Heart*, 116.

with me. In fact, I don't need to do that because I am so confident of the truth that I'm communicating to him, and I am even more confident that the Holy Spirit will do a better job of confirming the truth to him. But I am expecting that he will behave respectfully to me. I am expecting that he will not roll his eyes or try to get the last word in, etc. If he does argue back, rather than try to convince him of my position one more time (perhaps shouting even louder, "It is stealing!"), I will address the disrespectful behavior. If he responds, "Well, no one else would call that stealing," I would say, "You are acting disrespectfully by continuing to disagree and trying to get the last word in. If you continue to be disrespectful, the consequences will be . . ." and I would lay out (and implement) the appropriate discipline (see examples in chapter seven on "Make a Boundary").

As parents, we take our responsibility to "train up our children in the way they should go" seriously (Prov. 22:6). We are charged with the awesome task of teaching our children the truth. But this effort often becomes a power encounter.

I know a young man whose teacher gave him detention for spitting on the girl in front of him. His father asked him what in the world he was thinking. The young man said, "I didn't spit. I gleeked." His father was unfamiliar with the term but wasn't necessarily interested in his son elaborating. But the boy did so anyway. "Spitting is when you get a mouthful and force it out. Gleeking is when you just open your mouth and move your tongue slightly so that a little spray comes out."

The young man was certain that his punishment was undeserved, for he did not spit. All parents at this point need to decide how important it is to elicit agreement from their children that they are right, and their children are wrong. How important is it to you to hear those words?

It is not within my power to make my son agree with me. I am wise not to put my hope in things that are not within my power. Since I cannot *make* anyone agree with me, I ought to try to accomplish something else. So if my son insisted that he gleeked, and did not spit, I would say, "Gleeking is a form of spitting, and it is disrespectful. It is also against the rules, and if you do it, you deserve to be punished." Stating the truth and the consequences is within my power, but eliciting acquiescence is not.

Reality television now offers a spectacle over which we can ponder the ideology behind parenting. Shows like Super Nanny and Nanny 911 offer an occasion for my family to discuss what out-of-control children need. According to the expert nannies, what disobedient children "need" is sleep, time to think (in a thinking chair or thinking spot), and time to "cool off."

But in reality, what children need is the same thing we all need—to hear the truth about their sin so that they can repent. Sleep will not lead to repentance. Cooling off will not lead to repentance. And thinking (without teaching) is sometimes the last thing children need; it is thinking that got them in trouble. They need someone to speak clearly the truth about their actions, including the consequences. To ensure the voice of the Holy Spirit is not drowned by your voice, this word of truth should not be clouded by your emotional appeal or your demands.

Once I overheard my college-aged son enthusiastically explain to our younger children, "When you are in college, you don't have to attend your classes." I could sense this was a sweet revelation for him, but it was a disturbing one for us. I was tempted to use threats about a gloomy future or to employ shame or logic to convince him otherwise. I was tempted to appeal emotionally, invoking the frustration of paying for classes that he would not attend. But, instead, I said, "While you may not be required to attend, your grades will reflect your attendance." This was a non-demanding, non-emotional explanation of the truth and the consequences involved.

Not long after, he realized that grades and attendance go hand in hand. This type of lesson doesn't need a forceful, emotional appeal for change. I merely echoed the truth that was made evident to him in a multitude of other ways.

TEACHING FOR RELATIONAL CHANGE IN THE WORKPLACE

Dirk felt that he needed to address a concern with one of his employees named Vicki. She had been giving potential clients the impression that what they were asking was "too much" and that it was going to be a "big deal." He gently told Vicki that she could be more positive, and she responded as if he had criticized her for all her work that she had ever done.

She said, "I'm getting the impression that you think I can't do anything right. You think I'm always turning clients away."

Dirk wanted to be an empathic listener, so he acknowledged how she felt. But he was disappointed that his correction was met with this "nuclear response," as he put it. If this was how she was going to respond to gentle admonition, then she clearly wasn't very open to criticism. But Dirk also felt sad that any previous affirmation had been overshadowed and unnoticed.

Dirk had several options here. He could have listened more to how Vicki was feeling; he could have repented for his critical attitude; or he could have appealed to Vicki emotionally by expressing that her reaction made him sad or frustrated.

But Dirk believed that it was important for Vicki to know the truth about the situation. He had made it a point to affirm her work often, and this was the first instance where he was critical. So the next day, he said to her, "I have been intentional about affirming your work on a daily basis."

We can't judge whether this was the best plan of action by results, but, in this case, the results were positive. Vicki said, "I had not noticed, but since you say that, I will be more open to receiving it."

One of the students in my wife's second grade class stole five dollars from another teacher's desk. The janitor discovered Carlos was the culprit and made the boy give the money back to the teacher.

When Carlos returned to class, my wife said, "You are so lucky the janitor caught you!" Understandably, there was a look of confusion on Carlos' face, so my wife continued, "Otherwise you might have been able to keep the money." Now he was even more confused. Kristina explained, "Then you would feel guilty, rather than looking back on this day as the day you almost stole."

In an effort to get this boy to change, my wife had very few options available. She wasn't the appropriate teacher to discipline him, since he stole from another teacher. Pleading with him would likely have had little effect. And if she said, "Stealing is bad," he wouldn't learn anything he didn't already know. So she instructed him on what she knew about the way God made his heart. She showed him that he would feel guilty if he stole money and didn't get caught.

TEACHING FOR RELATIONAL CHANGE IN FRIENDSHIP

Allie plays tennis with her friend Tina once a week. They have been friends since they were young, but now they are both married, so this is their special time together. Tina is evidently unsatisfied in her marriage, and she uses this weekly meeting to vent her frustrations. Because Tina is having a hard time, she assumes that Allie approaches her marriage with the same attitude and has the same need or desire to air her frustrations about her husband.

Allie is hesitant to participate, but Tina doesn't catch on, so she tries to get her started. Tina "primes the pump" by saying things like, "Your husband is a hermit," or "You have to hold everything together in your house."

If Allie wants to put a stop to what she called "rag sessions," she can pursue any of the nine options in this book. Truthing would be a good place to start. She can say, "Our conversations about our husbands could be more encouraging." There is no emotional appeal, though we might guess that she is frustrated, disappointed, or uncomfortable. There is also no demand for a response—just a statement of the truth.

WHY THIS OPTION IS UNIQUE

In the introduction, I offered criteria for how to choose among the nine options for change. I stated that there is no right or wrong option in any given situation, nor is there a hierarchy of effectiveness.

For the most part, that is true. But the option of teaching is first in this book for a reason. It is the only option that goes at the top. I am partial to this option.

In parenting, especially, we must be partial to teaching. All of the other eight options for relational change serve the purpose of teaching. Our role as parents is to "train up a child in the way he should go" (Prov. 22:6). We are, as Tedd Tripp puts it, "the shepherds of our children's hearts." So when we listen, we do it to teach. When we make a boundary with our children, we do it with the purpose of teaching. When we compromise, we have teaching in mind. We only "leave" if it serves an instructional purpose. We sacrifice because we think it is an effective way to teach. We never "do nothing" because it is easy, but because it is instructive. Our emotional appeals are a form of teaching. Our own repentance with our children must be authentic, but it is also an instructive example.

To a lesser extent, this all holds true for other relationships. Proverbs 27:17 says, "As iron sharpens iron, so one person sharpens another." We do have an instructive role in each other's lives. We are, in a sense, our "brother's keeper" (Gen. 4:9).

All relationships offer an opportunity for teaching, but parenting and marriage have an inherently instructive purpose. That's why teaching is the priority of these nine options for relational change. That's why *teaching* is the first and longest chapter of this book. So while the other eight options for relational change follow in no particular order, it is intentional that teaching is first.

The criterion for choosing among the other eight options is always, "What is in the best interest of the other person?" But I offer an amendment to that question in this chapter. It is, "What is most instructive for the other person?" Speaking a word of truth may be most instructive. On the other hand, listening may be the best way to instruct. Perhaps leaving is the most instructive, or maybe connecting emotionally or one of the other options for relational change is best. Regardless of what you choose to do, each option for relational change serves to instruct.

CHAPTER 2

APPEAL

LET'S GO BACK TO MARIE. She could try appealing to her mother emotionally. She probably shouldn't unload all of the statements below in one sitting, but she could appeal to her mother in one of the following ways:

- "I feel disgusted when I go in this bathroom."
- "I feel frustrated because it seems like we have an unfair arrangement."
- "I feel exhausted because it seems like you don't help with the workload."
- "I feel concerned because it seems like you are unaware of the problem."
- "I feel ignored because it seems like my prior requests to get help from you have not worked."
- "I feel frustrated because it seems like I am cleaning this bathroom alone."
- "I feel anxious when I walk into the bathroom because it seems disgusting."
- "I feel exhausted, because it seems like we keep having this same conversation."

If I suggested to Marie that she make an emotional appeal, I can envision her saying, "But it won't work. I've tried it in the past."

First, we don't know that it won't work. It may be that today the timing is just right. Her mother or sister may be open to listening this time. Maybe her message will get through, either because of her persistence or because today is her lucky day.

Second, she may think she has tried this in the past, but maybe she didn't make her appeal as clear as she thinks she did. Perhaps in the past, she was sarcastic, "blew up," or made threats. But unless she made a concerted effort to communicate her emotions with skill, the chances are she did not get through.

We all know making an emotional appeal can be difficult because even the most careful, clear, and skillful communication can break down. For instance, one of the teachers at the school where my wife works placed a 911 call that failed to gain a response from the police, despite the teachers' frantic demeanor.

"We need you to come; there is a dog on the roof!"

"There's a dog on the roof, Ma'am?"

"Yes, and he is aggressive!"

"And he's on the roof?"

"Yes, and we are worried about the kids."

"The kids?"

"Yes, the kids are going to be heading up to the roof for recess in a few minutes, and there's an aggressive dog up there."

Now, what the teacher didn't tell the police was something so obvious it was taken for granted by everyone at the school: the school was built underground, and the roof is the playground—unusual, to be sure, but not to the teachers and students at that school. The point is we all think we know how to communicate, but we aren't as good as we imagine. We could all benefit from brushing up on our communication skills, which includes making an emotional appeal.

DEFINITION OF "EMOTIONAL APPEAL"

"A response seeking to connect with another person emotionally."

This appeal follows a fairly strict formula: I feel _____ because it seems like_____ now.

Perfecting our emotional appeals is vital for our sanity and for the preservation of our relationships. We all know that people who keep their feelings "bottled up" eventually explode, while those who express their emotions more consistently may have fewer explosions.

Pastor Tom Holladay explains, "The heart always leaks out. It's like the irritating high-pitched sound of air leaking out of a balloon. Some of us are quite good at holding negative feelings in for a while. The balloon keeps getting bigger and bigger; but along comes the slightest irritation and— blam!—your heart explodes out. Your emotions don't have to inevitably lead to an explosion. Give the feelings of your heart priority, and act immediately."[18] We make emotional appeals for the sake of our own emotional health. If these appeals successfully affect the other person's behavior, then count yourself doubly blessed.

Developing the skills of emotional appeal also ensures more successful communication. I have a friend who generally airs his frustration with sarcasm. The problem with this technique is that I rarely know what he is frustrated about or what he wishes had happened. I can sense the sarcasm, so I assume he is frustrated. But I don't leave

18 Holladay, *The Relationship Principles of Jesus*, 111-112.

the conversation with any helpful information for self-reflection. I just leave the conversation thinking, "That was weird." By perfecting your emotional appeal, you will probably discover that many of your previous attempts to communicate were not very effective or clear.

John Gottman provides some advice for beginning an emotional appeal. He characterizes a harsh startup versus a soft startup and recommends, "Soften your startup."[19] We know that timing and tact can go a long way in making an emotional appeal valuable. "A soft startup doesn't necessarily have to be this diplomatic. It just is to be devoid of criticism or contempt . . . discussions invariably end on the same note they begin. That is why 96 percent of the time I can predict the fate of a conflict discussion in the first three minutes."[20]

Ultimately, whether someone else hears you is up to them, not to you. We cannot take responsibility for the choices other people make. But you can make it easier or more difficult for others to hear you, depending on how you make your emotional appeal. The outcome is not completely in your control, but you can increase your chances of success by careful communication.

When we consider the option of making an emotional appeal, there are several reasons that we hesitate. We fear that it won't make any difference. Maybe the other person won't care how we feel. Or even if they care, maybe they won't change their behavior. Maybe sharing our emotions will just begin an argument, and the other person will just get mad.

But in truth, an emotional appeal is vital to the health of your relationships. We all deeply desire emotional connection—to know

19 Gottman, *The Relationship Cure*, 69.
20 Gottman, *The Seven Principles for Making Marriage Work*, 161.

others and to be known by them. So even if the other person doesn't change his behavior, at least he will know you better. And even if the other person gets mad, at least you did the right thing. Making an emotional appeal is not the only strategy, but it is an absolutely vital element of relational well-being.

One reason that an emotional appeal is vital is that it sets an important example. When my children were young, it was obvious that emotional appeals did not always have an immediate effect. For example, when my son was entering his pre-teen years, at times I told him that I was angry, and he had a blank stare on his face. He tried his best to communicate to me that he couldn't care less. Nevertheless, I knew that sharing my emotions with him was an important educational tool. It helped him mature by teaching him that we have emotions and that these should be shared verbally. It sent the message, "This is what relationally healthy people do."

Eventually, he developed the ability to make the type of emotional appeal described in this chapter. But the effect was not noticeable in the short term. Making these emotional connections is a long-term investment in the relationship and in the discipleship of the other person.

Emotional appeals teach people to think emotionally. Beyond the initial educational value of showing someone "this is what healthy people do," you have the opportunity to help the other person become more empathic. By making an emotional appeal, you help the other person remember that relationships are two-sided. You offer them a chance to put themselves in the shoes of others and consider how they might be feeling.

These appeals offer your friend a chance to connect with you. Emotional connection is not just educational; it is a gift. You offer a part of yourself. Emotional connection is unique from the other options for relational change explored in this book because it is inviting. You invite the other person in.

Emotional appeals maintain your important sense of self, your right to feel as you do. It is entirely possible that the other person may get angry if you tell them you are frustrated. Or they may act unfazed. In either case, you have preserved your dignity, and by expressing your emotions, you have refused to be minimized or dismissed.

Finally, emotional appeals are just the right thing to do, even if they don't have the effect that you had hoped. They are the right thing to do because they are an act of love. They require vulnerability and self-revelation, which are expressions of love.

NEGATIVE COUSIN TO EMOTIONAL APPEAL

As a teenager, I worked at a fundraiser with my twin brother to benefit our Boy Scouts organization. We were flipping Philly cheesesteaks at a church, and we were the only scouts who showed up. Fortunately, several adults were there to work the grill in that hot kitchen.

But like many of the other teens who could have been there that Friday night, we, too, had other things to do. So after about an hour into the four-hour event, my brother and I announced that we had to leave. One of the leaders became about as angry as I have ever seen anyone behave. In addition to having a red face, sweating, and pacing, he yelled, "You're leaving? Fine! If you leave, I leave!" Then he threw his spatula on the ground and stormed out.

As a 17-year-old, I really had no idea what the problem was. My brother and I looked at each other, walked to the car, and wondered, "What is he so mad about?"

Later that night, one of the scout leaders called us to explain, "Jim was angry because the adults are doing this work for the youth, and the scouts are not doing their share of the work. He didn't want the kitchen crew to be all adults on behalf of the kids."

In retrospect, this all makes sense to me; but the scene illustrates how ineffective an emotional outburst can be at communicating one's actual thoughts and emotions. Because we are, by nature, self-centered, even the most emotionally intelligent people are incredibly dense and averse to introspection. Our own actions and words always make more sense to us than the actions and words of others. Hinting, beating around the bush, and sarcastic jibes do not pierce the heart and leave people feeling convicted of sin. They only leave people wondering why you woke up on the wrong side of the bed.

Emotional fits rarely break the will of others or cause people to repent. In fact, they often have the effect of making other people feel justified because now they can prove how irrational your other demands, points, and emotions were. If you really want to communicate your emotions, you must master the skills in this chapter.

A similar, but less productive, form of emotional appeal is to "make a case." We should not confuse "telling how we feel" with "making a case."

I asked a young man to tell his wife how he felt after a particular incident, and he started, "First of all, I work really hard at my job, and secondly, I keep my mouth shut about a lot of things that bother me, and thirdly . . . " I could tell he was going to make a case but would miss the opportunity to tell how he felt.

It can be tempting to give an explanation for why we did what we did. Sometimes we make a case to prove that the way we feel is justified and to get the other person to approve of how we feel. While these explanations contain emotional outbursts, they do not help us to connect emotionally. They are actually cognitive explanations. They do not reveal how we feel, only what we think. Obviously, there are important and beneficial times to explain what we think. But doing so will not help you connect on an emotional level, and connecting emotionally may be what your relationship needs in order to get unstuck.

Another negative cousin to emotional appeal is "yelling and screaming." People make the false assumption that if they yell and scream, they are somehow more authentic and either more effective at communicating or at creating change. Truthfully, however, we often leave people guessing when we have emotional outbursts.

HOW TO MAKE AN EMOTIONAL APPEAL

Notice the format of the emotional appeals I suggested above:

- "I feel frustrated because it seems like I am cleaning this alone."
- "I feel anxious when I walk in the bathroom because it seems disgusting."
- "I feel exhausted because it seems like we keep having this same conversation."

In each of these statements, I have carefully followed four rules of emotional appeal:

- Say "I," not "you";
- Feel [emotion], instead of saying "feel like" or "feel that";
- Express how it seems, not how it "is";
- Use "now," not "always" or "never."

These rules require some explanation. First, talk about how *I* feel, what *I* notice, what *I* am thinking, and what *I* see. Don't make "you" statements. These statements, no matter how carefully made, have an accusing tone when offered in the midst of conflict. It may be tempting to talk about "you," but the purpose of the emotional appeal is not to punish or accuse; it is to connect. You want the other person to know you better, so talk about yourself.

Secondly, if you are making an emotional appeal, your statement needs to contain an *emotion*. I have observed that when people start a sentence with "I feel that . . . " or "I feel like . . . ," it is not often followed by an actual *emotion* word. Take the emotion "angry," for example. We never say, "I feel *like* angry" or "I feel *that* angry." What normally follows the words "like" and "that?" Thoughts, not emotions. Someone might say, "I feel like you are an idiot," or "I feel that you are being unfair." Neither of these statements expresses emotions. They express thoughts—accusing thoughts to be exact. Begin the statement with "I feel," and then supply an emotion such as "angry, frustrated, surprised, exhausted, overwhelmed, etc."

By carefully choosing a word that expresses an emotion, you will ensure that you connect emotionally with your friend. Since emotions belong to you and your perceptions, this language is less threatening and less arguable. No one can deny how you feel.

Thirdly, talk about the way it *seems*, not the way it *is*. The purpose of the emotional appeal is to improve the relationship. You are trying to de-escalate things from reaching a full-blown argument. You want the other person to connect with you emotionally. You cannot control the response of the other person, but you can make it easier or more difficult for them to connect with you. You can remove the hurdles to communication.

One way to remove the hurdles, and make it easier for the other person, is to restrict your appeal to the way it seems. Imagine, for instance, that you told your close friend, "We don't spend much time together." This is a perfect set-up for an argument. You have just challenged the other person to name the date and times that you have spent together in the last week. You put them in the position of having to prove you wrong, presumably so that you don't have to argue anymore and so that they don't have to be the "bad guy."

But if you say, "I feel disappointed because it seems like we have not spent much time together this week," the other person cannot disagree with you. Who can argue with the way it seems to you? Besides, you didn't accuse the other person of anything; you just stated that you are disappointed.

WHY SHOULD I PUT THIS MUCH WORK INTO IT?

People rightly recognize that employing the skills in this chapter is time-consuming and requires a great deal of effort. One client once asked me, "Why should I put this much work into speaking? Why not just say what comes to mind?" This man was coming to me for marriage counseling, and I wanted to say, "How's that working for you?"

Clearly, one answer to the question is that "just saying whatever comes to mind" is keeping the relationship stuck. The extra effort is worthwhile because it is disarming. It is also affirming the other person's feelings. You achieve more precision and greater understanding from the other person when you open a window for them to listen by being gentle and positive. Your words are also more accurate when you take the time to think through them and to communicate. Also, you make fewer disputable statements, which are bound to become distractions from the main point that you are trying to get across.

HOW MUCH DO YOU FEEL IT?

Having taken the time to carefully state how you feel and how it seems, it is sometimes helpful to add how much you feel that way. I can feel mildly frustrated or severely frustrated. Sometimes I am sorely disappointed, and other times I am slightly disappointed.

Les and Leslie Parrot write:

> Rate the intensity of your feelings. We have observed that one partner in the couples we counsel is often more expressive than the other. In other words, one person articulates his or her feelings more quickly and more intensely than the other. And we have seen this imbalance cause problems time and again because what is very important to one person may appear not to be very important at all to the other."[21]

Sometimes, adding the intensity of your feelings can easily end an argument. You were disappointed that your wife changed her mind about going to a movie. But she is feeling exhausted. Then you add that you are extremely disappointed (an eight on a scale of one to 10), and she says that she is mildly exhausted (like a three on a scale of one to 10). Once she hears *how* disappointing this is to you

---

21 Parrott, *Saving Your Marriage Before It Starts,* 130.

and compares it with her own feelings, she quickly changes her mind again and agrees to go after all. (May all your arguments end so favorably!)

WHAT ABOUT BEING A ROBOT?

I am convinced that following these four rules is vital for effective emotional appeals. But "following the sentence-forming rules" can seem inauthentic or contrived, since it forces us to speak in formulas. In fact, when my wife began practicing these communication skills, she averred, "I don't want to be a robot."

One reason she was put off by the "robotic" notion is that it seems unnatural to communicate feelings (which are deeply intuitive) in a formula. In addition, she worried that sharing her emotions in this way would negate the intensity with which she felt anger, frustration, elation, surprise, etc. She had a good point. When someone feels surprised, they don't generally say, "I feel surprised." They say, "Wow! What on earth? Oh my goodness!" If we feel rage, we don't generally say, "I feel rage." We raise our voice and make statements that are filled with rage. The fear of sounding like a robot, however, was short-lived for my wife when a friend of ours said, "What about, instead of thinking that you sound like a robot, you think of it as sounding *self-controlled?*"

Following the rules for emotional appeal does not make you a robot; it helps you maintain self-control. Similarly, we worry that following these rules will hide the intensity of our emotions. But how effective is the other strategy of just saying whatever comes to mind? Impulsive statements may be authentic, but they aren't necessarily effective at communicating either. They don't really explain why you feel as you do, what you want instead, or how things seem to you.

HOW BIG IS YOUR EMOTIONAL VOCABULARY?

One reason people don't make emotional appeals is that they lack a large emotional vocabulary. It wouldn't take you very far if the best you could do is say, "I feel sad" or "I feel happy." That would indeed be "robotic" and fairly ineffective.

As you practice making emotional appeals, also try to increase your emotional vocabulary. Here is a short list to begin building a vocabulary that evokes relational change:

ANGRY	FRUSTRATED	UPSET	ENRAGED
DISAPPOINTED	SURPRISED	MINIMIZED	NEGLECTED
ABANDONED	HOPELESS	LONELY	DISCOURAGED
FOOLISH	ISOLATED	EXCITED	EAGER
PLEASANTLY SURPRISED	CONTENT	PROUD	ECSTATIC
REGRETFUL	DEPRESSED	HEARTSICK	MISERABLE
DISSATISFIED	EXASPERATED	ENRAGED	DISTURBED
TERRIFIED	HORRIFIED	APPALLED	OFFENDED
SICKENED	DISGUSTED	APPRECIATIVE	AMUSED

DO PEOPLE REALLY DO THIS?

When I coach couples to practice these communication skills, they inevitably ask me, "Do people really do this?" At first, to some it seems silly, overly-thought-out, too formal, or just plain exhausting.

But the answer to the question is, "Yes." People really do talk this way. And it's not just marriage counselors or people practicing their marriage counseling skills. Perhaps in American culture in the past, families did not practice these skills often. We would admit that women have done a better job than men, but few of us have really followed the guidelines in this chapter. But that is changing.

The last century of psychological research and the emergence of self-help books and professional counseling have bequeathed a generation that is looking for and finding better communication skills. Dr. Gottman encourages, "I believe the emotionally intelligent husband is the next step in social evolution."[22]

The tools for better communication are available, and people are increasingly having higher expectations in their marriages. Typical, "normal" people are practicing the skills in this chapter, and they continue to follow the formula for an emotional appeal for decades into their relationships.

Admittedly, the formulas for communication in this chapter can come across as "robotic" and, therefore, as insincere. Exercising the self-restraint required to abide by these guidelines makes people feel that they are not giving their emotions honest reign in the conversation. Gottman observes:

> Many, if not all, of these phrases probably sound phony and unnatural to you right now. That's because they offer a very different way of speaking with your spouse when you're upset. But their phoniness is not a reason to reject them. If you learned a better and more effective way to hold your tennis racket, it would feel 'wrong' and 'unnatural' initially, simply because you weren't used to it yet . . . Over time they'll come easily to you, and you'll modify them to more closely suit your style of speech and personality.[23]

---

22 Gottman, *The Seven Principles for Making Marriage Work*, 109.
23 Gottman, *The Seven Principles for Making Marriage Work*, 173.

It is worth the effort and discipline to develop better communication skills, even if it seems unnatural at first. Eventually, you will see that even if you didn't display or vent your emotion enough, you still will have communicated your emotions in a way that is easier for the other person to understand. Flipping your lid, shutting down, flying off the handle, or checking out weren't serving you well before. These techniques have not left your friends and family wondering what they could do differently in the future. And these displays of emotion (or lack of) have not helped others know you better—other than that they need to be careful of you. But with more precise, self-controlled language, you will see that your emotions are actually communicated better.

WHAT EMOTIONAL APPEAL LOOKS LIKE IN THE BIBLE

We find emotional appeals throughout the book of Psalms. One of the functions of the Psalter (and of prayer) is to give an expression of every human emotion as we cry out to God.

Psalm 6:2-4 says, "Have mercy on me, Lord, for I am faint; heal me, Lord, for my bones are in agony. My soul is in deep anguish. How long, Lord, how long? Turn, Lord, and deliver me; save me because of your unfailing love."

In Psalm 22:1 we read, "My God, my God, why have you forsaken me? Why are you so far from saving me, so far from my cries of anguish?"

The ancient worshippers knew how to express a wealth of emotion when they spoke to God, and we benefit from their model.

There are numerous other emotional appeals in the Bible. One prominent and touching instance is in Esther 8:3: "Esther again pleaded with the king, falling at his feet and weeping. She begged him to put an end to the evil plan of Haman the Agagite, which he had devised against the Jews." Esther appealed to her new husband, the king of Persia, on behalf of her people. He was compassionate toward her, and in response, he caused the adversary, Haman, to hang on the gallows, which were intended for Esther's cousin, Mordecai.

Some people mistakenly assume that God is non-emotional, presumably because God is either "too rational" for emotion or because God is immutable. But one of the reasons we speak of God as a "person" is that He, too, has emotions, thoughts, and desires.

In Zechariah 1:3, God makes an emotional appeal: "Therefore tell the people: This is what the LORD Almighty says: 'Return to me,' declares the LORD Almighty, 'and I will return to you,' says the LORD Almighty."

We learn in Ephesians 4:30 that the Holy Spirit has emotions: "And do not grieve the Holy Spirit of God, with whom you were sealed for the day of redemption."

All this is to say that God does have emotions, and the Bible records God's emotional appeals. Here are some notable times God expressed emotion:

- Ezekiel 23:18 says, "When she carried on her prostitution openly and exposed her naked body, I turned away from her in disgust, just as I had turned away from her sister."
- Nahum 3:6 says, "I will pelt you with filth, I will treat you with contempt and make you a spectacle."
- Deuteronomy 1:37 says, "Because of you the LORD became angry with me also and said, 'You shall not enter it, either.'"

- Amos 5:21 says, "I hate, I despise your religious festivals; your assemblies are a stench to me."
- Isaiah 1:14 says, "Your New Moon feasts and your appointed festivals I hate with all my being. They have become a burden to me; I am weary of bearing them."
- Matthew 3:17 says, "And a voice from heaven said, 'This is my Son, whom I love; with him I am well pleased.'"
- Ezekiel 16:43 says, "Because you did not remember the days of your youth but enraged me with all these things, I will surely bring down on your head what you have done, declares the Sovereign LORD . . . "

Consider the emotions God displays in these verses—disgust, contempt, anger, hatred, weariness, pleasure, rage. Most likely, these words exceed your own emotional vocabulary. In each of these instances, God expresses a desire and an intention for relational change. We can create relational change by following God's example of a developed emotional appeal.

John Gottman is an expert teacher on how to make an emotional appeal. His approach is recognized by therapists worldwide, and his terminology defines the process. Gottman boils down the emotional appeal to one simple word: *bid*. A bid is an offer. When you make a bid, you are vulnerable because you are always offering something and hoping to get something in return (which may or may not come to fruition).

Gottman writes, "Even our best efforts to connect can be jeopardized as a result of one basic problem—failure to master what I call the "bid"—the fundamental unit of emotional communication."[24]

---

24 Gottman, *The Relationship Cure*, 4.

A bid can be a question, a gesture, a look, a touch—any single expression that says, "I want to feel connected to you." A response to a bid is just that—a positive or negative answer to somebody's request for emotional connection.

At the heart of almost every human connection is an emotional bid. Gottman gives a few examples of pithy communications we may be inclined to disregard, but even these are emotional bids.

For example, consider the following exchange:

"Did you call your sister? She seemed really down last time."

"No, I haven't. What do you suppose is wrong with her?"

Gottman contends that this short exchange is not merely small talk; it is an attempt for one person to have an emotional connection with the other person in the room. Such desire for connection even includes mundane exchanges like, "How about that weather?"

I have explained to my kids that when I ask, "What are you playing on your iPod," I do have a motive. I'm not simply trying to gather information, judge, or suggest something else. I ask simply because I see a child, whom I love, connecting with a small screen; and as time passes, I want to connect, too. I bid for emotional connection.

Very mature and secure people can begin to see critical statements and angry statements as fundamentally "bids" for emotional connection as well. Rather than simply hearing the obvious criticism or anger, we can look deeper and remember that the other person wants to connect. I say emphatically again—at the heart of every human interaction is the desire for emotional connection. Next time your partner says something frustrating or irritating, remind yourself that every communication is a bid for emotional connection.

After recognizing this consistent desire for emotional connection, Gottman suggests how we can respond to bids. We have three options: turn toward, turn against, or turn away.

Think of an auction. When you raise your paddle, you want the auctioneer to say, "I see that bid." You feel slighted or frustrated if he doesn't see it. And if you really want the auction item, you get louder and more obnoxious until your bid is recognized. That's what we all want from our emotional bid. We want the other person to say, "I see that bid." But we can do even better.

Now think of a game of poker, where you get the opportunity to say, "I not only see your bet, but I raise it." When my wife says, "I feel like the house is messy," she wants me to see her bid. And then she wants me to raise her bid by saying something like, "It sounds like you feel the house is a disaster. How can I help?"

Gottman's research indicates that we misread the emotional bids around us. "In one study researchers found that mothers misread their fussy babies 70 percent of the time."[25] If nurturing mothers misread the rather limited needs of babies that often, what hope do we have in correctly understanding the variegated emotional bids of complex people around us?

We must expect, assume, and prepare for the fact that we will not often hear or correctly understand the other person's bid for emotional connection. That's why this chapter aims not only to make a case for emotional appeals, but also to give four clear, memorable rules for making an appeal that will be correctly received.

Gottman recognizes that we all have varying degrees of fluency with emotional bids because we come from different backgrounds

---

25 Gottman, *The Relationship Cure,* 26.

where families deal with emotions differently. Gottman identifies four basic "emotional heritages." Chances are, you could readily determine whether your childhood home was "emotionally coaching," "emotionally dismissing," "emotionally disapproving," or "laissez faire."[26]

If your family of origin was "emotionally coaching," you have a head start in understanding the bids of others and making your own. If it was "emotionally dismissing," you'll need to learn how to identify bids and your own emotions. If it was "emotionally disapproving," you'll need to accept the legitimate and healthy role that emotional bids have in relationships. And if your background was "laissez faire" [hands off, uninterested] about emotions, you'll need to navigate the extremes of being emotionally "out of control" and being dismissive of emotions.

Finally, in your emotional appeal, be conscious of your facial expression, touch, and body language. Ironically, even though you are making an emotional appeal, you don't need to *act* emotionally. Your words convey your emotion, and, to be genuine, your body and face will have congruence with what you are feeling and saying. But just because you are frustrated, you'll have more success at connecting with the other person if your face does not betray utter contempt. And needless to say, though you are enraged, your body language should still convey an inviting stance that calls the other person toward you, rather than pushing them away.

---

26 Gottman, *The Relationship Cure*, 26.

WHAT EMOTIONAL APPEAL
LOOKS LIKE IN MARRIAGE

When we had small kittens, they had a special affinity for the feeling of leather scratched by their sharp claws. They especially liked our leather couches. I complained about it every time I saw a new scratch. I kept a mental note of the pattern of scratches, so I could identify new ones, and I let my wife know each time. I'm not sure what I expected to happen, nor was I aware of how upsetting this was to my wife. Finally, she said to me, "I'm feeling crazy because of your complaints about the couch. I feel powerless because I don't know what can be done about it. I feel trapped because I don't think we have any realistic options."

I realized that she was feeling blamed, but there was nothing we could do. The only real alternative was to get rid of the cats (which she was against). I didn't love the cats, but I love my wife more than the couch. Yet I had made her feel that I valued the couches more than I valued her. Her emotional appeal painted the picture I needed in order to understand what I was doing.

A client once told me that he doesn't share his feelings with his wife because nothing good ever comes of it. He said, "Your feelings are just there, and you can't do anything about them, so what's the point of talking about them? It just gets everyone upset."

I dispute his view on emotions for several reasons. First, I take issue with his approach because I think sharing emotions is unavoidable. You do have emotions, and your spouse will figure them out.

Second, sharing emotions is important because it is an act of love. The loving act flows both directions. Self-revelation is an act of vulnerability and is, thereby, an act of love. Intentionally making oneself vulnerable is an act of love.

In addition, when you share your emotions, you send a message to the other person that they matter. You validate the other person and, thereby, love them. Emotional appeals, therefore, are a gift. They are a gift of vulnerability from yourself, and they are a gift of affirmation to the other person.

Coming to this realization had a profound impact on my own marriage. I thought that I had become skilled at relational change, that I had perfected the appeal. And I fancied myself the "socially-evolved, emotionally-intelligent husband." Nevertheless, I grew weary with the feeling that I was always the one making an apology *first.* I wondered, "When is Kristina going to be the first to apologize?" I certainly asked her, "Why don't you ever apologize first?" But it never occurred to me to ask, "How do you feel about my apologies?" I realized that what I truly wanted and what I thought I wanted were two different things.

On the surface, I wanted to prove my point. But in a deeper sense, what I truly wanted was intimacy. Intimacy could be achieved by many routes, including my initiating an apology, asking how Kristina felt about my apology, or asking any number of other questions besides the accusation, "Why don't you go first?" The difference between these questions is connection and disconnection. The emotional appeal offers an opportunity for connection, which is what people are seeking in marriage.

Third, connecting emotionally can create relational change. In the book *Connecting,* Larry Crabb writes:

Ordinary people have the power to change other people's lives. An older priest can revitalize a despairing younger colleague by pulling the troubled man's head to his chest. A distraught father can touch his son with an energy that cuts through a hardened heart and awakens what is tender and true within the child. An adult daughter can offer something from hidden places within her to her aging mother that releases hope in the elderly woman's heart, hope that can support her through her loneliness, confusion, and pain.[27]

No matter the condition of your relationships today, they can each be deeper, richer, and more satisfying if you connect emotionally. This connection is created by a successful emotional appeal.

DOING IT "RIGHT"

You can improve your chances of connection by what you say. For example, let's assume your partner has pestered you about being on time to some event, and he calls to see if you have already left the house. Instead of saying, "Don't treat me like a baby," you can improve your chances of connection by saying, "I feel patronized when you call to see if I have left the house." But remember that this book is not intended as a rule book for you to consult to see whether your partner is playing by the rules. The advice is for *you*.

So even if your partner doesn't "do it right," remember that the goal is connection. Try to hear what it would have sounded like if your partner made a clearer emotional appeal. If your spouse complains, hear the complaint as a bid for connection. Admittedly, trying to read between the lines can be nearly impossible. Gottman asks:

> Does this mean that to read one another's bids, we have to read one another's minds? Obviously not. That's impossible.

27 Crabb, *Connecting*, 31.

Nor does it mean that we have to tolerate abusive expressions of rage or frustration just because they can be interpreted as bids for connection. But our research shows that a little understanding can go a long way toward uncovering the bids for connection that often lie beneath people's masks of anger, sadness, or fear. And once a bid is recognized, we can start the work that brings people together—the work of turning toward.[28]

You may not know exactly what your partner was trying to say (especially if they don't say it "right"), but you do know what your partner is trying to do. Your spouse is making an attempt at connection.

My wife once said to me, "You never listen to what I say." As I became a more experienced listener, I knew Kristina was making an emotional bid. I wasn't exactly sure what she was feeling, but I knew that my choices were to "turn toward, turn away, or turn against."

I decided to turn toward her, and say, "It sounds like you are feeling angry." She thought for a few minutes and finally admitted that she just needed to cry, and she wasn't sure why.

Feelings of anxiety or anger need to be directed at something. By becoming more perceptive at listening to emotional appeals (no matter how poorly formulated), you give your spouse the opportunity to direct that anxiety or anger at some other object besides yourself.

WHAT EMOTIONAL APPEAL LOOKS LIKE IN PARENTING

When my daughter sins, I have a variety of options. As her father, my primary responsibility before God is to instruct her. As I stated in the chapter on teaching, all of the other options for relational change

---

28 Gottman, *The Relationship Cure*, 36.

serve that central purpose. Part of that instruction includes teaching her to connect with me emotionally. I want an emotionally-intelligent child, a girl who grows up to be an empathic person. As a parent, an emotional appeal might sound like:

- "I feel concerned because it seems like you are lying to me."
- "I feel exhausted because it seems like you are demanding too much from me."
- "I feel attacked because it seems like you are accusing me."
- "I feel worried because it seems like you are not going to get your homework done."

Some parents may feel that it is inappropriate to make an emotional appeal to children. One objection I have heard is that children are too young to understand or to practice this sort of appeal.

Another objection is that an emotional appeal is irrelevant theologically. In other words, some say that children should obey simply because you are the parent, not because you feel sad. This is a very important point, and it raises a caution parents must heed: the purpose of an emotional appeal should not be to *get* obedience. That would be manipulative. Such a use of emotional appeal is, indeed, theologically irrelevant. Your child should obey because God commands it, not because you are frustrated. In addition, using an emotional appeal to get obedience is futile. It doesn't work. In fact, no action you can do guarantees obedience, so all attempts are futile, since your child's actions are beyond your control.

The purpose of emotionally appealing to children is threefold:

To instruct. As long as your emotional appeal is not the rationale you are offering for why your child should obey, these appeals are actually an important form of theological instruction. A carefully worded emotional appeal is a form of the type of instruction offered in the last chapter. This emotional appeal is speaking the truth about the situation, without demanding a response. You are instructing your child that among other things, your emotions are the consequence of their actions. Finally, these emotional appeals are self-controlled, so they are, in an ironic sense, "less emotional."

To connect. Your children deserve an emotional appeal from you because these appeals are an act of love. Your emotional appeal is an offering of self—even when it is rejected or when it doesn't result in a change of behavior. It is a vulnerable act and a gift (so long as it is not demanding of a response). As you offer these appeals, your children will connect with you, whether you notice or not. Regardless of whether you effect an immediate change, your child hears the appeal and does connect with you (and you with them). To fail to make these appeals is a form of protection and isolation and a way to offer less of yourself.

To model. Emotionally appealing to your child, following the formula in this chapter, will provide your child with a model that they can follow. This is not an unrealistic expectation, even with children two years of age. I will never forget when I heard my two-year-old daughter say, "I feel 'trated [frustrated] cuz it seems like nobody likes me." You can do your children a favor (and their future spouse a favor) by setting them decades ahead of the curve and teaching them to make emotional appeals now, rather than in marriage counseling.

With teenagers and adult children, emotional appeal becomes one of the most realistic options because you have fewer boundaries that you can establish as children get older. My 19-year-old son was coming home late at night—sometimes at two in the morning. We did not have a set curfew, but we did ask that he update us every hour after midnight where he was and when he was coming home. When he failed to do this, there were some boundaries that we could draw. We could refuse to pay his car insurance, or we could eventually ask him to leave the home. But we also thought it was instructive and important to appeal emotionally. My wife did not need any urging to do this because the situation was very troubling to her. One night he came home late, and my wife said, "I feel terrified when you don't tell me where you are at night."

I have stated that every human interaction is a bid for emotional connection. This is true with children—even when they misbehave or irritate you. In *Parenting from the Inside Out*, Daniel Sigel and Mary Hartzell provide this example of the ever-present desire children have for emotional connection:

> Imagine your child comes in from playing in the backyard very excited about the colorful beetles he's collected in a small open glass jar. "Look, Mommy, look what I found. Aren't they pretty?" All you see is the possibility of bugs loose in the house. "Get those creepy things out of here right now," you say sternly . . . In this situation, the child's emotional experience was totally missed.[29]

If the desire for emotional connection is ever-present, then so are the opportunities. By seeing irritation, and even sin, as an opportunity for emotional connection, you and your kids will gain a richer experience from what would otherwise be neutral to negative interactions.

---

29 Sigel and Hartzell, *Parenting from the Inside Out*, 58.

WHAT EMOTIONAL APPEAL
LOOKS LIKE IN FRIENDSHIP

Connecting with people emotionally is a gift of friendship. But making emotional appeals can be scary because it may create confrontation, but at the same time, you are also expressing to your friend that you value the friendship enough to make it more authentic.

Years ago, I worked with a woman who sent terse emails, usually requesting something of people. She didn't express appreciation, and she usually added some comment like, "You are over budget," or "You need to fix this." Because email is a one-dimensional form of communication (you can't see, hear, or feel the person), statements like this are usually taken as neutral to negative.

After receiving several of these emails, I wrote back to her, explaining, "When I read these mails, I feel anxious because it seems like I am in trouble." I added, "I feel hopeful because I believe there is a more positive way."

Historically, confrontation with this coworker escalated her negative attitude. But I think that is because people rarely connected with her emotionally when they confronted her. People had told her that she was wrong, or they told her what they thought, but they did not often tell her what they felt. When I made an emotional appeal, she responded with an apology. Then she did something unprecedented: she sent an email simply encouraging me that a project I worked on was well done.

CHAPTER 3

LISTEN

ANOTHER WAY THAT MARIE COULD untrap herself from the unhealthy relationship with her mother would be to listen. She has made some assumptions about why her mom won't clean the bathroom. And she has tried some strategies to get her mom to help out, but none of these has worked so far.

If she listens, she may find out some key information. She may discover what is causing the mental block in her mother or what's misfiring in this relationship. By listening, Marie may be able to identify and then remove some hurdles to change. Even if Marie doesn't learn some new, vital information by listening, her mother will feel loved. This would be progress. Given the current, static nature of her situation, even a small change here would be an improvement.

The reason we must listen is that we can be woefully unaware of what everyone else around us knows. I recall one time when I drove to the bank and walked up to the ATM that everyone was exceptionally cheerful. *Everyone* smiled at me. I thought this was weird. Then on my drive home, someone pointed at me and smiled. I was very puzzled and almost disturbed. So I marched in the front door and yelled, "What's funny about me?" My wife said, "Do you mean the princess tiara you're wearing that your daughter made for you?" I had forgotten that before going to the ATM, my six-year-old put this on my head. Apparently, it was too comfortable to notice!

None of us is as good as we think we are at knowing what others are thinking or feeling. To get untrapped, we must listen.

DEFINITION OF LISTEN

"The hard work to see the world the way the other person does."

THE SILENT TREATMENT: A NEGATIVE COUSIN TO LISTENING

One of the negative cousins of listening is "the silent treatment." We give the other person a triple dose of listening—in that we aren't going to say anything to them. Maybe we're afraid we'll lose control if we talk, so it's better to say nothing at all. More likely, we just ignore the other person because we don't want to listen to them or see them. This is partly punishment and partly protection. We hurt too much to be around them, and silence seems safer. Gottman gives an example of this type of relationship:

> Think of the husband who comes home from work, gets met with a barrage of criticism from his wife, and hides behind the newspaper. The less responsive he is, the more she yells. Eventually he gets up and leaves the room. Rather than confronting his wife, he disengages. By turning away from her, he is avoiding a fight, but he is also avoiding his marriage. He has become a stonewaller.[30]

---

30 Gottman, *The Seven Principles for Making Marriage Work*, 33.

Gottman's image of a stonewaller is expressive: a person as silent and impenetrable as stone and as insurmountable as a wall. In other words, this is a person who "shuts down" in the midst of conflict.

Another negative cousin to listening is interrogating or "launching an investigation." Chloe and Will were separated for a few months after Will entered rehab for alcohol addiction. During that time, she developed a phone/texting relationship with another man. She texted the new boyfriend and called him several times a day. They would talk for an hour each evening before she went to bed, and he sent her text messages that said things like, "Good morning, Babe."

Will eventually discovered this relationship, and, for obvious reasons, he was threatened. He interrogated Chloe, "Where did you meet him? Why did you text him so often? How often did you meet with him? Why was he calling you 'Babe'? How many other people do you know who call married women 'Babe'? Don't you think that's strange? Can't you see how this looks suspicious to me? What were you doing when you were on the phone with him? Did you ever refuse to answer my calls because you were on the phone with him?"

Will mistook interrogating for listening. He lost sight of the fact that the purpose of listening is to connect, not primarily to gather information (and least of all to build a case).

WHAT LISTENING LOOKS LIKE IN THE BIBLE

A distinctive trait of the God in the Bible is that He is always listening to us. The preoccupation of many religions is how to get God to listen. Christians believe that God is always near and always watching.

In Exodus 3:7 we read, "The LORD said, 'I have indeed seen the misery of my people in Egypt. I have heard them crying out because of their slave drivers, and I am concerned about their suffering.'"

Why does God listen? Surely it is not to collect more information. God already knows everything, past, present, and future. And God doesn't listen just to catch us in some error so that He can pour out judgment. He listens because He loves us. Listening is an act of love.

Listening is also wise. We read in Proverbs 18:13, "To answer before listening—that is folly and shame." If we fail to listen, we not only make fools of ourselves, but we also leave a wake of damage in our relationships.

James 3 speaks of the tongue as a "restless evil," set on fire by hell. The author observes how people have been able to tame every animal in the world, but not the tongue. He compares the tongue to a small spark that sets a forest ablaze and to a tiny rudder that controls a large ship. All this is to say, "Everyone should be quick to listen, slow to speak, and slow to become angry" (Jas. 1:19b).

HOW TO LISTEN

There are so many good books on listening that I do not need to give a long treatment to the subject. Instead, I offer just a few skills here and a short discussion.

Good listening requires empathy. Many people assume that empathy is a feeling of compassion, where you imagine how you would feel if you were in someone else's shoes. In this sense, the skill required for empathy is a good imagination. In reality, however, empathy is discovering how the other person actually *does* feel in their shoes. The skill required is not imagination, but determination.

Empathic listening is often characterized by these four questions:

- What was it like for you when . . . ?
- How do you feel about . . . ?
- What would it mean if . . . ?
- What thought went through your mind when . . . ?

It really does matter how you word your question, so it is worth writing these four questions on your heart.

Imagine, for instance, a couple discussing whether or not to move out of state. Let's say Jack wants to move because he has a better job opportunity, but Jill wants to stay where they are now. If Jack wants to listen, sensing that Jill is resistant to the move, he can ask some questions. He could also make a case for the move, make an emotional appeal, manipulate, etc. But assuming that he wants to listen, his novice attempt at listening might begin with questions like these:

- Why don't you want to move?
- What are you afraid of?
- Can't you see this is important to me?
- Don't you care about our finances?
- Haven't I been supportive of things you want to do?
- Are you mad at me?

If Jack asked these questions, he may not realize that Jill will probably feel threatened. Here are some possible reasons why she would feel threatened:

- *Why don't you want to move?* Jill may wonder, "Am I OK? Am I allowed to feel this way? Did I say I didn't want to? I was just not sure about it; I didn't realize I was actually against it."
- *What are you afraid of?* Jill may wonder, "Is my fear stupid?"

- *Can't you see this is important to me?* Jill may wonder, "Does my disagreement mean that I am against him?"
- *Don't you care about our finances?* Jill may wonder, "Does my reluctance to move make me less responsible?"
- *Haven't I been supportive of things you want to do?* Jill may wonder, "Am I being unfair by disagreeing?"
- *Are you mad at me?* Jill may wonder, "Am I allowed to be mad? If I say 'no,' then I'm not being honest, but if I say 'yes,' I will be in trouble."

The purpose of listening is to *invite*, rather than *repel*. The questions above don't come across as inviting. Jack could still ask almost the same questions above with some important modifications. By making these adjustments, Jack can invite Jill close to him, rather than prompt her to protect herself, withdraw, or become defensive. Jack's more experienced attempt at framing questions to engage in listening might produce questions like these:

- What thought went through your mind when I said I wanted to move?
- What would it mean for you to live in another state?
- What is it like for you to know that this is important to me?
- How do you feel about our finances right now?
- How do you feel about my level of support for you now?
- How do you feel about me right now?

If most of us were better listeners, we wouldn't need a list. We could develop our own set of questions and pave our own way. But in reality, most of us are such bad listeners, we really do need a set of time-honored rules to help us succeed.

I have listed four suggested questions for empathic listening, four rules for emotional appeal (chapter two), and four rules for teaching (chapter one). Some people feel constrained by rules and don't like being put in a box. They wonder how seriously they should take the idea that there is a finite set of questions they can ask or statements they can make. So I want to make it clear that these are not technically rules; you can do whatever you want.

This isn't a moral issue, as if you sin by putting your emotional appeal wrongly. Nor are these prophetic rules, as if I am declaring the demise of your relationship if you say the wrong thing. The rules are not transactional, as if your partner gets the right to ignore you if you "say it wrong." Your relationships can handle the stress of you saying the wrong thing (and your partner saying the wrong thing to you). In fact, your relationships can handle a great deal of this stress if you often follow it with resolution or forgiveness.

Instead of thinking of these sets of questions and statements as moral rules, think of them as pragmatic guidelines. I am offering a way for you to increase your chances of success at becoming untrapped from negative patterns. I am illustrating a way for you to remove the hurdles that stand in the way of the other person hearing you. You are not responsible for the actions of another person, and you are not capable of controlling their response. But you do have a great deal of influence. While you cannot make someone be mad at you or not be mad at you, you can make it a lot easier for them to get angry at you, and you can make it easier for them to stop being mad.

Good listening requires that you ask questions. But there are several types of questions that are not intended for listening. Instead, these questions are a way to "make a point." David Augsburger has some suggested questions to avoid:

- The leading question that snookers: "Don't you feel that?" or "Wouldn't you rather . . . ?"
- The punishing question that scolds: "Why did you say (do, try) that?"
- The demanding question that imposes: "When are you going to do something about [that]?"
- The dreaming question that conceals: "If you were in charge here, would you rather . . . ?"
- The needling question that provokes: "What are you waiting for?" or "What did you mean by that?"
- The trapping question that ensnares: "Didn't you once say that . . . ?"[31]

Good listening requires asking questions. But not all questions are fair or productive. To be a listener who successfully connects, you must ask questions that invite, rather than investigate.

CAN I ASK "WHY?"

I was teaching a parenting seminar and addressed the topic of empathic listening. I explained to the group the four questions included here. One father asked, "Can we ask 'why?'" I'm not much of a legalist, but I simply answered, "No. It's not on the list. Stick to the four questions on the list."

In my counseling, I often suggest my clients should not ask, "Why?" At least, they shouldn't until they have lots of listening experience and have determined whether the "why" will come across

---

31 Augsburger, *Caring Enough to Confront*, 35-36.

as, "Can you tell me more about that?" or "How can you possibly have been so insensitive?"

The question "why" is unproductive for several reasons. First, it almost always comes across as an accusation. It implies that the other person has done something wrong, stupid, or senseless.

Secondly, "why" is a difficult question to answer. When you ask "why," it is uncertain whether you are asking, "What was your motive?" or "What series of events led up to this?" or "What was the decision-making process?" or "How were you feeling when you did that?" In other words, the other person doesn't know if you are connecting on a cognitive level or an emotional level, or if you are simply asking about the history behind the event. Often, the other person doesn't know the answer to the question "why" anyway.

Finally, especially when addressing children, the question "why" is something the parents are more prepared to answer than they are. Ask a three-year-old why he hit his brother. He doesn't know why. He doesn't know the answer, but you do. He hit his brother because he sins, just like you and I do. Now, what you really meant to ask was, "What precipitated this conflict?" But that's a bit over a three-year-old's head. Sticking to the format of the four questions I listed above, you could ask, "How do you feel about your brother?"

Children don't know why they steal cookies from the cookie jar. But we do. They steal because "the heart is deceitful" (Jer. 17:9). It is not a child's job to determine his motives; it is your job as the parent to teach your children what God's Word says about the heart.

As an alternative to "why," I would suggest asking:

- Can you tell me more about that?
- Can you tell me what happened?

- Can you tell me what you were thinking beforehand?
- Can you tell me what series of events came before that?

These questions are more disarming. They don't put the other person on the defensive, and they don't require the ascription of motive. These questions are better than the question "why" because they are more precise in communicating the type of information you want to understand.

GET AT THE CORE

Often in the midst of conflict, we tend to focus a great deal on behavior without hearing what beliefs, values, and fears are driving that behavior. One year, as summer began, I asked my wife about our plans for taking a trip. I asked her, "Are we planning to go away for a couple weeks?" She replied, "No. I don't feel like it." I was crushed, angry, frustrated, and shocked. I just walked away appalled, feeling like she had just ruined my summer and taken away one of my motivations for working the rest of the year. I came back and asked her about it, and she said, "I was just feeling overwhelmed." I should have known better when she first said, "No."

Behind every action, there is a value. Behind that value, there is a belief. And with that belief, there is often a fear. Take my wife's proposed action, for example, of not going on vacation. Behind that action, there is a value. In this case, we might suppose she values sanity, peace, relaxation, and relieving stress. Forming those values are beliefs. She believes that peace of mind is an important thing. Behind that belief, there is a fear. She also believes (at this time) that if she goes on vacation, she will have more anxiety than if she stays home. She fears that too many things will pile up when she is gone and that the vacation will earn her no relaxation because she will just have to work twice as hard when she gets back.

When she said "No" to going on vacation, I should have tried to find out what value was leading to that decision. And I should have considered what belief led to that value. I should have asked her what fears she had about going. Chances are, we could have a big argument about whether to go on vacation, the whole time feeling like we are at odds with each other. But I share her values. I, too, value relaxation, peace, sanity, and relieving stress. I share her belief that peace of mind is an important thing. And I even share her fear that if we go, things will pile up.

In order to get my way, I could begin making a case. I could prove to her that there is nothing to fear. I could argue that going on vacation will be more relaxing than staying at home. I could promise to help with any work that piles up. In short, I could try to remove all the justification for why she feels the way she does.

That strategy will fail on two counts: it won't build intimacy in our relationship, and it won't convince her to change her mind. By removing her justification for feeling as she does, I actually communicate something I don't believe. I send her the message that I don't share her values because I invalidate what she is saying. It is one thing to not share another person's behavior, but it can feel quite threatening to sense that someone you love doesn't share your values or beliefs.

A better strategy is to determine which values, beliefs, and fears are at play and discuss those. Better yet, find common ground and express how you share the same values, beliefs and fears with the other person. That way, the other person does not need to defend their values as aggressively because they sense you are on their side. Find a solution that honors both people's values. I am determined to go on vacation, while my wife is opposed to the idea. It is entirely

possible that we go on vacation while honoring her beliefs and values or that we stay home while honoring my beliefs and values.

The importance of digging deeper into the realm of values, beliefs, and fears is apparent with more complicated and serious scenarios. Curtis had a drinking problem, which was disturbing his wife, Ellen. For a couple years, she focused solely on his behavior. She asked him to drink less, to drink less often, and to not drink at all. He conceded at times to these requests because he knew his drinking was causing a great deal of stress in their relationship.

In counseling, she explained that she just couldn't see why he didn't give up drinking altogether. Why would he keep doing it if it made her so uncomfortable? "Is drinking really more important to him than I am?"

I told Ellen that it may be difficult, and even infuriating, but she might want to offer an empathic ear to him. Certainly, his road to recovery would take more work than empathic listening, and I wasn't implying that she bears any blame for his addiction. But I believe nearly every situation presents an opportunity for empathic listening, and this loving act can create relational change. Besides, she had already tried several of the other options for relational change that I've suggested in this book but to little avail. So what did she have to lose by trying empathy?

Eventually, Ellen mustered the courage to ask some difficult empathetic questions: "What do you *value* about drinking? What do you *believe* about drinking? What do you *fear* will happen if you don't drink?" Curtis told her that he feared not being an enjoyable person to be around if he stopped drinking. He believed that he was boring and offered little to others when he was sober. He believed he was a more likeable, social, funny, and interesting person when he was drunk.

Curtis faced months of difficult recovery after Ellen asked him those empathetic questions, but he did remain sober and saved his marriage. Many other choices contributed to his sobriety, but the questions his wife asked provided an opportunity for self-reflection that Curtis had not experienced before.

WHAT LISTENING LOOKS LIKE IN MARRIAGE

Jerry and his wife, Melissa, were discussing with me a recent disagreement. They live near Disneyland, where many people have annual passes and special discounts for being local residents. Melissa said that because of financial problems, she was thinking of getting the lowest level of passes, which would restrict them from going to the park on weekends. Jerry shook his head and said, "That's the first I ever heard of that." It was obvious that he was against the idea. I could see that I was about to get my own free ticket to an attraction— a fight—but this attraction would not be amusing.

I explained to Jerry, "Your goal is not to get the better passes to Disneyland." Jerry was confused.

He asked, "It's not?" I could tell he was pretty sure I was wrong.

I said, "Your goal is intimacy with your wife. If you try to prove your case, both of you will dig in your heels and become defensive. Use this opportunity to know your wife. See it the way she sees it. Ask her why she wants these passes, what it would mean for her if you didn't get them, what she is afraid will happen. Get into her world and know her."

Jerry and Melissa needed to ask the basic question, "What is the purpose of this relationship?" Is the purpose to save money, enjoy entertainment, overcome loneliness? When we are clear about the purpose of the relationship, many of the other issues become clear as well. When we affirm that the purpose of marriage is to build intimacy, then we are mindful that disagreements are opportunities to know the other person better. When Jerry and Melissa asked God what the purpose of their relationship was, they learned that they could be used by God as vessels of intimacy for one another.

The idea that the primary purpose of marriage is intimacy is made clear in the beginning of the Bible. We read in Genesis 4:1, "Adam made love to his wife Eve, and she became pregnant . . ." It's no surprise that Adam lay with his wife or that sexual union has been central to marriage since the beginning. But interestingly, the word translated "lay with" is the Hebrew word *Yadah*. Literally, *Yadah* means "to know." If you read Genesis 4:1 in the King James Version, it says, "And Adam knew Eve his wife; and she conceived . . ." Both translations of *Yadah* are accurate.

The general word "to know" is often the one supplied for sex. This is not merely a euphemism, as if the biblical authors were afraid to use the real word for sex, so they substituted it with a euphemism. There's plenty of explicit material in the Bible to show that the authors didn't have qualms about the precise words for sex. When sex is equated with "to know," it is because the concepts are similar in the mind of the author.

Sex is a way to know someone, to create intimacy. This is to say that intimacy is the goal and purpose of marriage, and sex is one action that serves that purpose. But there are additional ways to create intimacy, and empathic listening is one of the best.

Glynn told me during counseling that his wife, Jen, swore at him and called him names the night before. He wasn't sure how to respond. This book offers nine positive options among which he can choose and a criterion to help make the decision. The criterion is, "What is in the best interest of the other person?"

In this chapter, we are looking at the option of listening. It is possible for Glynn to listen when his wife swears at him. It might look something like this:

Jen: "You're an A--hole!"

Glynn: "You're feeling very frustrated with me right now."

Jen: "Yes, you never think about anyone but yourself."

Glynn: "I strike you as really selfish."

Jen: "You're the most selfish person I've ever met!"

Glynn: "Tell me more about when you've seen me act that way."

Jen: "You showed up last week at counseling late, with a Starbucks cup in your hand."

Glynn: "And what thought went through your mind when you saw that cup?"

Jen: "He has time to get himself a cup of coffee, but he can't get to counseling on time."

Glynn: "So you felt unimportant to me?"

Jen: "Like I was less important than a cup of coffee."

Think of how differently that conversation could have gone. Jen could have said, "You're an A--hole," to which Glynn may have responded, "You too!" And this might have been the end of the discussion, or it could have gone in a completely different direction. Instead, Glynn has an opportunity for connection. He can say, "I see that I have made you feel less valuable, and I'm sorry." This is a real win for the relationship. It is one more building block toward achieving intimacy.

WHAT LISTENING LOOKS LIKE IN PARENTING

As I mentioned earlier, when my son enrolled in his first college class, he came home and pronounced the good news to the whole family: "When you're in college you don't have to go to class."

"That's not exactly what they mean," I responded. I compared this to when a child asks a teacher about playdough, "What is non-toxic?" and the teacher says, "It means it won't kill you if you eat it." Then the child tells his friend, "It means you can eat it."

But my son insisted that he didn't need to attend class. Like many parents, I began envisioning a future set in stone with his absenteeism. He's going to fail all of his classes! He's not going to graduate. And what if this is his attitude toward work? He's never going to keep a job!

But at this point, rather than continue teaching him or appealing to him, I decided to listen. I asked him, "How do you feel about leaving class? What thought goes through your mind when you are sitting in class, and you think about leaving?"

Through this conversation, I learned something I never would have if I only tried to teach. It became apparent that his small group leader from church was putting a great deal of pressure on him to attend small group during one of his classes. The small group leader made it clear to him that this was more important than school. All of the other guys in the group were attending, and some were even coming, despite other commitments.

When my son told me this, I imagined what would have happened if instead of listening, I had simply said, "You have to go to class. Period. You'll never succeed with that attitude." These ultimatums shut people down, and they prevent knowing. If I had said that, my son would have closed up. He probably would have said, "OK," but in a passive-aggressive way. Without listening, we imagine that we are succeeding more than we actually are. Without listening, we imagine that others hold our same convictions more than they actually do. There is certainly a role for teaching, even if it shuts down dialogue. But this cannot be the only strategy or the only interaction that we have with our kids at any age.

In *Parenting from the Inside Out*, Siegel and Hartzell speak about the joy of listening to our kids:

> Every day we miss opportunities for making true connection because instead of listening and responding appropriately to our children we respond only from our own point of view and fail to make a connection to their experience. When our children tell us what they think or how they feel, it is important to respect their experience, whether or not it's the same as our own. Parents can listen to and understand their children's experience rather than tell them that what they think and feel isn't valid.[32]

Some parents may feel that they must choose between listening or teaching, but these are not mutually exclusive. Good listening cannot be done at the same time as teaching, but both practices are inherent to good parenting. Listening is a ministry to your children, with a blessing and joy in return. That blessing is greater connection and the offer of love that comes with listening.

My daughter Rebekah had a couple years in elementary school when getting dressed for school made her literally hysterical. She screamed, cried, and threw whatever type of fit you can imagine a five-year-old throwing. She often made us late because she refused to wear anything except the one outfit that was in the wash because she had worn it the day before. We attempted to solve this situation by picking out clothing the night before, so that she knew what she was going to wear when she woke up. I think she agreed at night with genuine intentions to obey. But she simply could not get in those clothes in the morning. We tried several options, some of which were reasonable and others which were immature responses. I took the

---

32 Siegel and Hartzell, *Parenting from the Inside Out*, 85.

other kids to school and left her with my wife, so that she would see how late her behavior was making her. I punished her. I yelled. And I told her that this reaction was ridiculous. None of this worked. I felt like anyone reading this book feels—trapped and out of options.

Finally, I had a revelation. She was willing to put up a fight about her clothing, even though she was absolutely clear that she was about to receive a particular punishment. Not getting dressed was worth it to her. If I had been inconsistent in administering the discipline that I had promised, I could see how she would call my bluff. But my wife and I consistently implemented the punishment we warned about in advance. So she must have calculated the cost of not getting dressed against the cost of putting on those other clothes. And she continually chose, instead, to be punished. This made no sense to me. Then it dawned on me—if this behavior makes no sense, maybe I should listen.

I am admitting here, I chose the option of listening because nothing else worked. I figured there was nothing to lose because it became apparent that her behavior was simply not going to change. I asked her, "How do you feel about your clothes? What thought goes through your mind when I say, 'Rebekah, get dressed'? What is it like for you to try on new clothes? What would it mean for you if I said, 'Let's go shopping for clothes'?"

She told me the clothes were itchy and too loose. I'm sorry to disappoint you because I'm sure you were hoping for a better explanation. But I was not primarily hoping for an explanation. That is not the main reason that I listened. I listened to love. If I thought there were an explanation, I would have heard it by then. The bottom line is that her experience of getting dressed in the morning fractured our relationship. We both felt unloved, and we both felt unloving during those mornings before school.

That needed to change more than anything else. It was far more important to me that she felt loved by me than that she wear a new outfit to school every day. I wasn't going to win that one anyway. I could not make her feel comfortable in her clothes. But I could make her feel comfortable in our home.

My wife and I recognized that much of this battle was motivated by our fear of being judged (for not doing the laundry or not buying enough clothes). This is not a noble concern for parents. And children are perceptive. They know what concerns us, whether it is embarrassment or whether it is discipleship. We abandoned the fear of embarrassment, but we did send a note to the teacher explaining that she would be wearing two outfits to school until further notice. Finally, she came up with a better solution; she would wear her other outfits on the outside of the clothes that felt comfortable.

As you listen to your kids, you may get better explanations than I got that day. Or you may not. This really is beside the point. As you listen, you will offer love to them.

WHAT LISTENING LOOKS LIKE IN FRIENDSHIP

Intimacy is not only for marriage. It is a worthy goal in every relationship. Jan is an adult woman, living with her mother. Her mother struggles with OCD (Obsessive Compulsive Disorder). Because of her condition, their relationship can be quite strained and is far from ideal or even typical. Jan told me that her mother often takes the things that Jan buys for herself and doesn't replace them (like food, toiletries, etc.). She felt violated and hopeless that things would change, even with confrontation. Generous people tolerate a certain degree of this behavior, but it can be frustrating when there is no reciprocation, acknowledgement of the problem, gratitude, or warning that your things won't be there when you need them.

I encouraged Jan that she may have misjudged the purpose of her relationship at this point with her mother. When she was a child, the purpose of the relationship was for her mother to care for and raise her. Now that she is an adult, Jan said she thought her current purpose was to be a good daughter. I suggested that throughout the stages of life, there are changes in the purpose of a mother/daughter relationship. Perhaps her current purpose is to serve her mother. Maybe it is to care for her as she struggles with her disorder. Maybe God's purpose is for her to know herself better. The ideal purpose for the relationship is for the two of them to gain intimacy as friends.

Jan is going to be perpetually frustrated if she does not know how God is using her in that relationship. Once she finds clarity on that question, she will have some way to deal with what is happening when she is offended in some way by her mom. In those situations, she can ask, "How does God want to use me in this relationship?" Then, rather than react as a victim, she can act intentionally as a vessel of God.

One important thing to keep in mind when listening is that, while gathering information is of some value, creating intimacy is the true goal. That greater goal is especially helpful in light of the fact that we often say things we don't mean.

I mentioned earlier that my wife, Kristina said, "You never are interested in what I have to say." I told her I was sorry that I had made her feel that way and assured her that this was important to me. Later, she said, "I was just feeling sad and wanted to cry." We both recognized that, sometimes, we have a generalized feeling of anxiety, anger, or sadness, and that feeling needs to find words to express itself.

And other times, those generalized feelings are expressed in non-verbal ways. For a period of a few months, one of my children awoke in the middle of the night and turned on all of the lights in the house. When we talked to him about it, he couldn't really offer an explanation, nor could he articulate his anxiety.

As we listen, it is valuable to keep in mind that what we hear may not be the clearest explanation, nor may the speaker be aware of the whole story.

I received a call from a member of our church named Lorna. She spent about 20 minutes complaining about a variety of issues. She had been on a committee to help remodel the nursery, and she didn't like that someone installed AV equipment in the room. She was bothered that blinds were installed without her consultation, and she didn't like the way the committee placed the furniture in the room against her advice.

After I hung up with Lorna, I asked another pastor on staff, "What should we do?"

He said, "That's a no-brainer. Call her up and love her! Have someone visit with her and listen."

Lorna was recovering from recent surgery. That's not an excuse for her negative attitude, nor is it a complete explanation, as I understand she may have legitimate complaints about the committee and the decisions. But her cancer treatment could not be dismissed any more than her specific complaints that she articulated. It is a pretty good part of the explanation for how she was feeling. I was awestruck by the other pastor's state of grace to see that this was a no-brainer, and I said to myself, "I want to be like that man!"

Similarly, another church member named Dwight dropped by and hurled accusations about each member of our staff. Again, I asked my friend, "What should we do?"

My friend's intuitive wisdom and grace proved true again: "He sees that many of his friends have moved out of the area, died, or have left the church, and he is grieving."

Again, Dwight's grief is not an excuse for the accusatory tone, and we should not dismiss his words by reading completely between the lines. However, we *must* read between the lines. In this instance, the lesson was that we must connect emotionally.

Dwight and Lorna called the church out of a desire to connect. What did they hope to accomplish by calling? I'm not sure how they would articulate it, but I doubt that the primary purpose was to have the nursery committee reconvene or to have a judge render a guilty verdict on our staff. They wanted emotional connection, or intimacy, which is best achieved by listening.

My friend Chris told me how he scolded his daughter for making a mess of her food all over her clothes and the floor, and then she ran to the arms of her mother for comfort. His wife cuddled the girl and comforted her. Chris said it made him angry that his wife consoled their daughter. I know why I'd be angry: "My wife is making me the bad guy. She's making me look mean."

I was just about to say something like, "Yeah, I would be too," and then continue under the assumption that we had understood each other. But I believe in empathic listening. So instead, I said, "Tell me

more about that anger." Because I make the assumption that everyone thinks like I do, I would never have predicted that his answer
would be so divergent from my own thinking.

He said, "I'm angry because she is a softie. I don't want the kids
getting away with everything." He was angry for a different reason
than I would have been, and I learned this by doing the hard work of
careful listening.

WHY WE DON'T LISTEN

There are various reasons why we don't listen. Sometimes we
think we already know the answer. Other times we feel contempt for
the other person. And at times, we simply don't care.

WE DON'T LISTEN WHEN WE THINK WE
ALREADY KNOW THE ANSWER.

When I was a teenager, I worked in a grocery store. Customers
would often ask where a particular item was located. They were often
in a hurry, so they would start speaking before they came close to
me. And they would continue walking in whatever direction, even as
I gave the answer. By the time I finished speaking, they would often
be out of earshot, not necessarily headed in the direction that I had
indicated. Since then, I have reminded myself, when asking for directions, to stop and wait until the other person has finished speaking.
Not only is it polite, but the fact that I asked for directions means that
I don't know where I am going!

We do this in our personal relationships all the time. We either
fail to ask questions because we think we know the answer, or we
barely listen to the answer because we think we understand as soon as
the other person starts talking. The truth is, you and I misunderstand

the people around us more often than we think and that includes the people we know best. We assume that the way we would feel in someone else's shoes is the way they feel, and we think this is empathy. Empathy is harder work than making that assumption. It is finding out how someone else feels and then feeling it yourself. Listening is hard work, and we like to find short cuts.

WE DON'T LISTEN WHEN WE HAVE CONTEMPT.

Sometimes we fail to listen because we are disgusted, and we have contempt for the other person. I have a friend, Jason, who is extremely organized, almost to the point of compulsive behavior. He thoroughly packs for a day and keeps everything he owns in perfect condition. Jason told me that he went to the zoo with his wife, Laura. They walked across the huge parking lot to the tram and were just about to board when she realized she forgot her hairbrush. She said she had to go back to the car to get it. It was a long walk, but both of them are in excellent physical shape, so it shouldn't have been a big deal.

But it was a big deal to Jason. It was about responsibility for him. He stood at the tram and waited while Laura walked back to the car to get her hairbrush.

I asked Jason, "How did Laura feel about walking back to the car alone?" Jason seemed surprised at the question. More pertinent to him was how he felt about her irresponsibility. Jason was reluctant to ask Laura this question because, despite their fairly healthy relationship, in this case he was too filled with contempt for her.

No one knows how to hurt you better than the people you love, so they may have the perfect jab or sarcastic comment to set you off.

Listening requires self-control to overcome the feeling of contempt or offense. But self-control can be learned and is worth the effort.

WE DON'T LISTEN WHEN WE DON'T REALLY CARE.

We also fail to listen because we don't want to hear the answer. In counseling, I observed a couple fighting about their approach to parenting. The wife, Jenna, expressed that her husband, Dave, was too harsh with the children. She said something like, "I would never act like you do to the kids. You're bossy and a bully."

When Dave heard this, he had a variety of positive options for how to respond. One option that he had not often considered, however, was listening. Since this was a skill Dave needed to work on, I suggested that he could ask Jenna to tell him more about this. "Can you think of a time when I came across as a bully? How did you feel about that? What would you like me to do differently?"

When I made this suggestion to Dave, the look on his face was revealing. He seemed to say, "I couldn't care less how she feels about it!" In fact, I asked Dave what it was like for him to imagine asking these questions to his wife, and he essentially said that he doesn't care how she feels.

One of the reasons that his listening skills were poor is that he didn't genuinely want to know. No amount of skill improvement can overcome that heart condition. If you don't want to know the other person better, you won't be able to convince them that you are becoming a better listener.

WHY LISTEN?

Just as there are reasons we don't listen, there are compelling reasons for us to engage in listening, if our goal is to be untrapped in our relationships. First, we listen to understand the people we're relating to. Secondly, we also listen to love. And third, we listen to heal.

LISTEN TO UNDERSTAND

How often do you think you misread people when you listen to them? When I have determined that I will do the extra work to listen to the other person, I have been amazed at the world of discovery that could otherwise have been left obscure. A pastor friend of mine, Albert, and I went out to lunch one time, and he told me that he had attended a local church where they sang the hymn, "Holy, Holy, Holy," with some revised words. The traditional wording is, "God in three persons, blessed Trinity." Albert told me that at this particular church they supplied the words, "God in His glory, blessed is He."

The first thought that went through my mind was "that's disturbing." And I assumed Albert was telling me the story because he was also equally disturbed. I had reason to make this assumption: Albert and I share much of our theology in common, and we often work together, so we can anticipate each other's thoughts.

I could easily have said something like, "That's disturbing," and left the conversation at that. No more would have been said about it, and we would go on to the next topic. But I am determined to be a more empathic person, and I know this means living with an ever-present mindset that I am misreading people. I must let them frame the picture.

So I asked Albert, "How do you feel about that?" Albert said, "I liked it. I don't believe in the Trinity." Now it is possible that Albert and I could have many conversations over the next decade without ever learning that important fact about him. He would likely have not offered it freely for fear of conflict. And I would likely not have asked, given my propensity (and everyone else's) to assume that the people around me see the world the way I do.

Careful listening leads to important discovery. This leads us to the conclusion that the value of empathy lies in gathering more information about others. And this is true, to some extent. If we want to offer advice, how will we know what advice is needed until we really see the world the way the other person does? If we want to help someone change his behavior, how can we know what help is needed until we accurately see the problem? But this is only a small part of the value of listening or empathy.

LISTEN TO LOVE

As I talk to people about becoming better listeners, it is apparent that many think the value of listening is only to gather more information. It is a mistake to assume that this is the only purpose of listening, as it robs us of many of the other benefits. If we think the main purpose is to gather information, then we are likely to stop listening once we are confident that we have correctly understood.

Another reason to be a better listener is simply to be a better lover. To listen is to love. When people feel understood, they feel loved. When they feel misunderstood or ignored, they often feel unloved.

When our adopted son, Sonny, first came to live with us at the age of seven, he had some habits from his previous home that were hard to break. He went to the bathroom and showered with the door open. We asked him to shut the door, but he failed to comply. I remember being awakened in the middle of the night to the sound of him in the bathroom with the door open, and I was enraged—partly because he disobeyed, partly because it seemed disgusting, and partly because it's just not what we do in our home, and it seemed weird.

But as parents often experience, sometimes no level of anger is enough to effect change in children. No amount or type of discipline, shame, or display of emotion seemed to be able to break the habit. What would cause a kid to go to the bathroom with the door open, knowing full well that an angry parent is around the corner about to come scold or discipline? I couldn't imagine the reason. But I've determined to become a better listener, so I ought to ask.

The next morning I found a non-threatening time and place to ask Sonny some questions:

- "What is it like for you to imagine going to the bathroom with the door shut?"
- "What thought goes through your mind when I say, 'Shut the door when you go to the bathroom'?"
- "How do you feel about having the door shut when you are in there?"
- "What would it mean if you were not able to have the door open?"

Through this conversation, I discovered that Sonny was afraid of the sound of running water. He worried that there were snakes or spiders that could come up out of the drain. This was a powerful and simple answer to the above question: "What would cause a kid to go to the bathroom with the door open, knowing full well that an angry parent is around the corner about to come scold or discipline?" Fear. Fear would cause a kid to do that.

Fear is an incredibly powerful motivator. It can keep someone from doing all kinds of things, even though he may be punished.

And it can cause someone to do all kinds of things, even though there may be negative consequences. At a subconscious level, there seems to be some calculation going on here, even with a seven-year-old. It's as if he is thinking: "I know I am going to get yelled at, but I'm certainly not going to shut that door. Keeping the door open is worth the punishment. Going to time out is better than getting bit by a snake that may come up out of the toilet."

Gathering this information was an important discovery for us, and as I explained above, this is one of the values of empathic listening. But in this case, there really isn't much I can *do* about this discovery. I can't ridicule the fear away, nor can I argue against the fear with logic. Asking these empathic questions serves a deeper purpose: Sonny felt loved.

Previously, when I disregarded his fear and went straight to scolding, he implicitly felt that his fear didn't matter (even though I was unaware of it) and, therefore, he felt unloved. Listening is an act of love in itself and, for that reason alone, has tremendous value. Even if listening effects no change in behavior, it ascribes value to the other person. That may not change behavior, but it changes the relationship.

Listening is a way of knowing, and knowing is the most profound act of love. In the account of Adam and Eve, we can vividly see the connection between knowing and love. In the King James Version, we read that, "And Adam knew Eve his wife, and she conceived . . ." (Gen. 4:4). I used to think the word "knew" was a euphemism, in order to make this Bible story suitable for children.

As I mentioned earlier, the Hebrew word here, *Yadah*, is used throughout the Old Testament for two different ideas: knowledge and sex. The biblical authors weren't looking for a tidy version; the Bible is filled with stories that many would consider unsuitable for children. The ancient Hebrew thinkers just equated knowledge with sex because both are a form of intimacy. Nakedness.

Being known is a deep human need, equal and similar to the need to be loved. We long for intimacy, and that is achieved by people taking the time to get to know us. As you sincerely listen, you say to your friends, co-workers, and family members, "I love you." This option for relational change will not cure everything. But it will lay a vital foundation of love for you to be able to move forward in other ways.

LISTEN TO HEAL

One valuable reason we listen is to heal. Being understood is therapeutic. Often, the only tool for healing for someone is through retelling their story to an empathic listener.

For example, what therapeutic plan is there for a victim of sexual abuse? Often, the therapist will recommend telling and re-telling the story. Through the empathic experience, there is healing.

Similarly, someone with anxiety can find healing as they explain to an empathic listener what goes through their mind as they face each situation throughout the day. Telling the story is often the best means for healing. If this is true for people who have major situations from which they need to heal, imagine the ministry you can have to the people in your life as you put forth the hard work to become an empathic listener.

Les and Leslie Parrott offer this advice for becoming better listeners:

> The point of reflective listening is to let your partner know that you have heard what they said and that you understand their message. By the way, reflective listening

is a wonderful way to defuse a potential conflict. If your partner starts hurling "you" statements such as, "You are always late," don't' say, "I am not." Instead, genuinely express your understanding of his or her feelings by saying, "I know it upsets you when I'm late. It's got to be exasperating. I'll work on being on time in the future." Listen for the message underlying the actual words. "You are always late" means "I'm upset."[33]

If we can listen enough to hear which "I feel" statement is behind each "You did" accusation, we will open a wide doorway for communication and intimacy.

DO I HAVE TO LISTEN EVEN IF I'M ANGRY?

When I urge people to become better listeners, they inevitably ask, "What if I'm angry?" They wonder if I am sentencing them to a lifetime of listening, without ever getting to respond, defend, or confront. Maybe you were wondering the same thing when you read the dialogue between Glynn and Jen, and you're thinking, "If I'm Glynn, when do I get to say what's on my mind?"

Becoming a better listener doesn't mean you never get to speak your mind again. But it might mean that you decided to do it tomorrow, instead of today. It is impossible to do the hard work of careful listening described in this chapter and also to speak your mind at the same time. But you always have tomorrow. In all of your relationships that matter to you (that would prompt you to read this book), you are in it for the long haul. You have a lifetime ahead of you where you can speak your mind and make your point. Most

---

33 Parrott, *Saving Your Marriage Before It Starts*, 89.

likely, you have done a lot of that already. But you could probably become a better listener.

As with all of the nine options for relational change, I am not saying this is the only way to respond to someone else in the midst of conflict. It is an important way, a loving way, and an effective way. It is also an often-neglected way and one that takes a great deal of self-control and determination. No one has to remind you to defend yourself or to speak your mind. You may, however, need a reminder to listen, and that's what I'm offering in this chapter. I don't argue that listening is superior to any of the other positive options, but it is a necessary part of the relationship.

How do you know when it is time to listen? I have offered the criterion in this book—when it is best for the other person. That's true enough for the nine options presented here, but listening is a little different. You really have so little to lose and so much to gain by making this a "default" option, at least to begin. If you plan to teach, listening will help you know the most pertinent thing to say. If you plan to appeal, listening may curb or reshape your emotions. If you plan to make a boundary, listening may help you do it more effectively.

The concepts of active listening are widely known, and many people are aware of basic rules like not interrupting, making eye contact, paying attention, watching body language, etc. As a result of the publicity that "good listening" often receives, many people envision a dichotomy between two kinds of people in the world—good listeners and bad listeners. This reductive dichotomy is unfortunate for a few reasons.

First, few people identify themselves as bad listeners. Since most of us overestimate our abilities, the dichotomy lets people off the hook because they have already identified with the good listening group.

Another reason the dichotomy is unfortunate is that good, active listening skills do not go nearly far enough in developing the intimacy aimed at in this chapter. While counseling, I ask clients to envision a gas gauge with empty, half-full, and completely full positions. In the empty spot, I place bad listening. In the midpoint, I place good listening. And in the full position, I present a third type of listening— empathic listening. This is not just watching body language, comprehending the situation, and restating or asking questions. Instead, empathic listening is a real desire to enter the other person's world and to do the hard, hard work of seeing the world as they see it.

CHAPTER 4

SACRIFICE

SACRIFICE IS ANOTHER OPTION FOR relational change in Marie's relationship with her mother. Marie could make a conscious decision from now on to joyfully clean the bathroom herself without expecting anyone else to contribute. She could decide (joyfully and willfully) that this is her lot in life. It will be her act of love to clean up after her mom. It is not sacrifice if she has no choice in the matter. And it's not sacrifice if she doesn't do it joyfully. But many people have made similar decisions to "bear the cross" for others as a precious, sacrificial gift.

This is not the only right way to respond, but it is a beautiful way. And it is well within our capacity to practice these gifts of sacrifice far more than many of us do. It will not go unrewarded. Jesus promises a reward—both in this life and in the life to come—for those who willingly suffer (Matt. 19:27-30). Those who make a habit of sacrifice know the reward begins immediately. As your capacity to sacrifice increases, your capacity for love increases. And as your capacity for love increases, you become a more joyful person.

DEFINITION OF "SACRIFICE"

"The intentional decision to suffer or act on behalf of someone else."

Pastor Tom Holladay explains:

> True love sacrifices. The greatest sacrifices may not be the once-in-a-lifetime sacrifices; they may well be the daily sacrifices. You give up your way and seek another person's good. No one else may even know you did it, but you'll know you acted in response to Jesus' love for you.[34]

Love is something you do, something you bring. Often, it comes in the form of a sacrifice. Amazingly, even though the sacrifice goes unnoticed, it can be a powerful tool for relational change.

VICTIM MENTALITY: THE NEGATIVE COUSIN OF SACRIFICE

Sometimes, those who sacrifice play the victim. If Marie's decision to clean the bathroom herself is not authentically sacrificial, it will fail to resolve conflict or produce change. The change that is worth pursuing here is not a clean bathroom, or a fairer distribution of work among her sister, mother, and herself. The change that sacrifice accomplishes is a more peaceful Marie. So if she cannot do it joyfully and without expectation, then she will end up only proving to herself how unfair her situation is. She will mount months of evidence (which she will surely keep track of) that proves she is the only one doing anything about the bathroom. Ironically, no one else will be interested in her case. She will only prove this to herself, and her sister and mother will end up thinking, "What's bothering Marie so much?"

WHAT SACRIFICE LOOKS LIKE IN THE BIBLE

The prime example of sacrifice in the Bible, of course, is Jesus. Jesus set the example in Isaiah 53:7: "He was oppressed and afflicted,

---

34 Holladay, *The Relationship Principles of Jesus*, 127.

yet He did not open His mouth . . . " Tom Holladay explains: "When
criticized, Jesus gave a clear, confident response. When honestly
doubted, Jesus offered proof. When ridiculed, Jesus was silent. When
backed into a corner, Jesus turned on the light. When rejected, Jesus
went elsewhere."[35]

In Jesus' sacrifice, He was not simply a passive victim, nor was
He a doormat or a punching bag. Jesus used sacrifice to create relational change.

The Bible commands us to imitate Jesus' sacrifice. In Philippians
2:3-8, we read:

> Do nothing out of selfish ambition or vain conceit. Rather, in
> humility value others above yourselves, not looking to your
> own interests but each of you to the interests of the others.
> In your relationships with one another, have the same mind-
> set as Christ Jesus: Who, being in very nature God, did not
> consider equality with God something to be used to his own
> advantage; rather, he made himself nothing by taking the
> very nature of a servant, being made in human likeness. And
> being found in appearance as a man, he humbled himself by
> becoming obedient to death—even death on a cross!

In 1 Peter 2:23, we read of the reason why Jesus was able to sacrifice with calm confidence: "When they hurled their insults at him,
he did not retaliate; when he suffered, he made no threats. Instead,
he entrusted himself to him who judges justly." Sacrifice is an act of
faith in the goodness, power, and truthfulness of God. We imitate
Jesus' example and obey the biblical commands to sacrifice because
we know that God's commands are good and that He is in control.

---

35 Holladay, *The Relationship Principles of Jesus*, 183-188.

In 1 Corinthians 6, Paul addresses the issue of lawsuits among Christians. He says that when Christians sue each other, it is a bad witness to the unbelieving world, and, therefore, both parties are already both defeated in what should be their primary goal.

Paul summarizes his argument with a profound question: "Why not rather be wronged?" You and I can both come up with some good answers to that question. "Why not rather be wronged?" Because it hurts. Because it's unfair. Because it is unjust. Because it is uninstructive to the other person to let them continue sinning and walking all over you. Because it is unhealthy to be a person who has no boundaries. These are all true objections and valid points. For that reason, sacrifice is not the only form of response, and it may not be the best or right option every time. But sometimes, being wronged may very well be the option that God is leading you to.

And even though all of the previous objections have some validity, there is plenty of reason to allow yourself to be wronged. Why allow yourself to be wronged? Because sometimes, the offense just doesn't matter that much. Because sometimes, our loss "is only money." Because often, allowing ourselves to be wronged is an imitation of Christ. Because suffering wrong is a powerful testimony. Because enduring is instructive to the other person about Christian priorities. Because relationships are more valuable than anything else.

In Paul's letter to the Romans, the apostle expresses his heart for his fellow Jewish people. He desires their salvation so deeply and regrets their inability to notice the Messiah so greatly, that he says, "For I could wish that I myself were cursed and cut off from Christ for the sake of my people, those of my own race" (Rom. 9:3). In other words,

Paul says he was willing to go to hell to save others. That is serious sacrifice! Even if it weren't a realistic possibility for Paul, he was exemplifying the selfless attitude of followers of Christ.

In Philippians, there is a well-loved statement from Paul, "I can do all this through him who gives me strength" (Phil. 4:13). This verse is often misapplied, as people take it to mean that they have power in Christ to accomplish great feats (which is true, but not the point of the verse). In verse 12, Paul says, "I know what it is to be in need, and I know what it is to have plenty. I have learned the secret of being content in any and every situation, whether well fed or hungry, whether living in plenty or in want." The point Paul is making is that in Christ he has learned and become able to make great sacrifices for the sake of the Gospel and for other people.

WHAT SACRIFICE LOOKS LIKE IN MARRIAGE

Jesus did not sacrifice for His bride (the Church) because she is a loser but because she is beautiful. Likewise, the husband must sacrifice for his wife because she is beautiful, not because she is less than him or a lost cause. Gary Thomas gives an excellent example of sacrifice in marriage:

> When I grew up, my family lived by a simple rule; if you take out an ice cube, you refill the tray before you put it back in. Now I'll pull out a tray and find nothing more than half an ice cube—which I call an ice chip. It was amazing how much such a small detail irritated me. I asked Lisa, "How much do you love me?"
>
> "More than all the world," she professed.
>
> "I don't need your love that much. I just need you to love me for seven seconds."

"What on earth are you talking about?" she asked.

"Well, I timed how long it takes to fill an ice cube tray and discovered it's just seven sec—"

"Oh Gary, are we back to that again?"

It finally dawned on me one day that if it takes Lisa just seven seconds to fill an ice cube tray, that's all it takes me as well. Was I really so selfish that I was willing to let seven seconds' worth of inconvenience become a serious issue in my marriage? Was my capacity to show charity really that limited?[36]

One important point that this story illustrates is that love is something you bring to a relationship, not something you get out of it. As a pastor, I have often heard people say, "I left that other church because I didn't get much out of church." I often retorted, "What did you bring?" Church is a place of worship, and worship is the act of bringing a sacrifice to Someone who is worthy. So the concept of getting something out of church is rather bizarre from a biblical perspective. In the Bible, we read of the things people brought: birds, grain, money, livestock, a hymn, a word of thanksgiving, a psalm, a work of prophecy, etc.

Gottman summarizes the concept of "sacrifice" in his "Principle 4: Let your partner influence you." He gives the following example:

Jack was considering buying a used blue Honda. The car seemed like a great deal since the seller, Phil, had only owned it for a month. He was ready to do the deal, but first he told Phil he wanted a mechanic to check the car. "Why?" said Phil. "It's really a new car. It only has three hundred miles and you get the manufacturer's warranty."

---

36 Thomas, *Sacred Marriage*, 94.

"True," said Jack, "but I promised my wife I wouldn't buy a car without having it inspected first."

Phil gave Jack a withering look. "You let your wife tell you what to do about cars?" he asked.

"Sure," said Jack. "Don't you?"

"Well, no. I don't—didn't. I'm divorced," said Phil.

"Well," Jack chuckled. "Maybe that's why."[37]

Most of us don't need to get our way all of the time. But it's nice to know that the other person is willing to give in some of the time. That's sacrifice.

I heard a pastor make the observation at a funeral that people are born into the world with their fists clenched and grabbing everything, but we die with our hands relaxed, outstretched, and holding nothing. It is our nature to fight for things, even things that we don't want, just because they are being taken away. This comes out in relationships when people start to fight over ideas, which they do not hold to as strongly as they come across, or to defend ground that they do not need or appreciate as much as they pretend. We do this because we want to know whether the other person is flexible or willing to sacrifice. Once we determine that the other person has no likelihood of budging, we are inclined to mirror that inflexibility. We do this partly because we want to know that we have influence on the other person.

Years ago, my wife started a party rental company with her father. I stayed out of the company and decision-making for the most part. But I did see that our money was on the line, and I wanted to know that I had some influence.

---

37 Gottman, *The Seven Principles for Making Marriage Work*, 99.

Sensing that I did not know my place in the decision-making, I became less flexible. She purchased a truck, some storage space, and a lot of other capital. They were about to buy a trailer, but I expressed concern over this much initial investment. Yet, I wasn't a director of the company, and they went ahead with the purchase despite my concerns.

At that point, I started to contest most decisions, even small ones. My wife and I discussed what was going on, and I realized that I needed to test my level of influence. I did not feel safe if I did not sense that I had any influence. Feeling powerless, I began to defend ground that wasn't even important to me. We both learned that once you demonstrate to another person that they can influence you, they loosen their grip. But as long as the other person senses they have no influence, the grip gets tighter.

As that grip tightens, we find ourselves defending ideas we don't really believe to the same level of intensity that we imply just to see if we actually have influence on the other person. Once you prove to other people that they can influence you, they loosen the grip of control, lessen the intensity of their argument, or widen their willingness to compromise. In other words, we are often subconsciously "putting out feelers" to see if we have influence. And when we sense that the answer is "no," we become unreasonable and angry because we feel backed into a corner and under-valued. You can use sacrifice as an opportunity to show other people that they have influence on you. Once they sense this influence, your sacrifice will have created relational change.

WHAT SACRIFICE LOOKS LIKE IN PARENTING

When my son, Sonny, was in high school, he forgot one of his textbooks at home, and he sent me a text message asking if I would bring it to school for him. This was rare. He was normally responsible about remembering his stuff, so I was surprised when I got the message. I had to think about how to respond, since it was a first for me as a parent. As I thought about the request, lots of parental aphorisms went through my mind: "If I do this for you, you will never learn to take care of yourself. You need to experience the consequences if you are going to become more responsible. If I rescue you in high school, who is going to rescue you in college?" But then it occurred to me, he already knows how to take care of himself. He doesn't need to become more responsible in this particular area. This is the first time I have had to rescue him.

So I thought about the criterion of the nine options for change: what is best for the other person? Among the nine options, I am clearly biased toward the first: teach. All of the nine options are valuable and worth consideration, but they all serve to teach—especially in parenting. Teaching is foundational; and if we decide to appeal, listen, sacrifice, do nothing, etc., it is only because we determine that this is the best way to instruct.

But when Sonny asked me to bring his textbook, it didn't seem like there was really any lesson for him to learn. He just needed help. So I brought by the textbook as a small sacrifice, simply as an act of love.

I have stated throughout this book that each of the positive options serves the fundamental purpose of instruction. Sometimes, sacrifice can be powerfully instructive, as a demonstration or example of Christ.

We have a family of seven, which we often try to fit in a minivan with seven seats. One of the captain's chairs in the middle has a car seat for the baby. That leaves one other captain chair for the four remaining children to battle over, and the three losers of the battle have to sit on the bench in the back. One particular morning when this scenario developed into an obnoxious fight among the kids, my wife said she would sit in the back bench in order to let one of them sit in the front seat, which is usually hers. This was an act of sacrifice. You may be thinking:

- That doesn't solve anything; the kids just got their way.
- They weren't punished for their fighting? (You think we should make a boundary.)
- You didn't teach them that they were being selfish? (You think we should teach.)
- Why not make a compromise and let them trade off? (You think we should compromise.)

Trust me, I had the same thoughts, as I'm sure did my wife. But this act of sacrifice is not our only positive option: it is one among nine. It is an option. And how well was punishment working for us, anyway? We've often asked the kids to sit in time out in the back bench quietly with their hands folded as a result of these fights. And we've tried multiple other types of discipline as well. Punishment hasn't "solved" the problem.

We've also done plenty of teaching about this particular scenario. We have told our kids, "You are being selfish. It is not loving to fight over your seat in the car. Jesus told us to take the lowest seat at the banquet so that the humble will be exalted. You are making your seat more valuable than your relationship with your sister."

We have also tried compromise. Micah gets the captain's chair on Monday and Wednesday ("W" is an upside-down "M"), Tasha on Tuesday and Thursday, Sonny on Saturday and Sunday, and Rebekah on Friday. We have tried boundaries, teaching, appealing, and com-promise—four of the positive options in this book. None of these strategies is powerful enough in one dose to eradicate selfishness. But a lifetime of relating to one another with an array of positive options helps us get closer to the goal.

When my wife sacrificed her seat for one of the kids, did it work? It depends upon what it was intended to accomplish. It did end the immediate fight, but that was never the goal. It did not eradicate all selfishness from our kids, but that wasn't her immediate goal either. And, admittedly, it did not accomplish repentance, which is an im-portant goal, but was not the goal of her sacrifice.

Yet her sacrifice did work. It accomplished what it was intended to do. It demonstrated the type of behavior that we had been in-structing our children to have all along. In many previous occasions, we had instructed them to be less selfish, told them that we expected them to yield their seats, and punished them for fighting over it. On this occasion, however, my wife demonstrated it. That demonstra-tion was also instructive.

Remember that the criterion for choosing among the nine posi-tive options is not "Will it work?" anyway. The criterion is, "What is in the other person's best interest?" Since my wife had already done a sufficient job of teaching, compromising, appealing, and making a boundary (discipline), she believed that sacrifice would be in our kid's best interest. This sacrifice would serve to instruct in a comple-mentary, but powerful, way, since it is the attitude of Christ that we are expected to share.

WHAT SACRIFICE LOOKS LIKE IN FRIENDSHIP

Gary Sittser explains the role of sacrifice in relationships in his book, Love One Another. He writes:

> Service means sacrifice. It requires us to give so that we learn to live with less (time, money, energy, opportunity, advancement), [so that] others in need will have more . . . The Bible teaches that servanthood is every Christian's duty . . . Jesus envisioned a community of disciples who would dare to move downward instead of upward, to retreat from ambition so others could get ahead.[38]

Sacrifice can be counterintuitive, can seem counterproductive, and can offend every sense about what we think is right. We will always be able to justify not sacrificing, and chances are our case will be strong. But strong doesn't always mean beautiful, and justified doesn't always lead to relational change.

Furthermore, as Sittser points out, sacrifice does not always need to be as painful as it seems: "No matter how difficult reaching out to others and carrying their burdens may seem to be it ceases to be a burden when the Lord turns it in to love."[39] I hope you are privileged to know at least one person who regularly sacrifices for others, without even realizing that this is what he or she is doing. Such a person doesn't even experience sacrifice as a cost because the pleasure is his or hers to be a conduit of God's love.

I firmly believe that sacrifice can be an instrument of relational change, but the change cannot be our central goal. Instead, simply representing Christ to the other person is the central goal. It would be manipulative to use sacrifice as a means of controlling someone

---

38 Sittser, *Love one Another*, 92-94.
39 Sittser, *Love one Another*, 131.

else's behavior, and thus it would cease to be a true sacrifice (selfless gift). In addition, we will be disappointed if we have unrealistic expectations. Sittser observes:

> Those who bear burdens should also remember that their burden-bearing is ultimately a matter of obedience to God's command, not a matter of utilitarian service to others. Not everyone with burdens will respond as we would like. They might take longer to overcome their problems than we think is appropriate. They might never overcome them at all. They might even take advantage of our helpfulness, exploit our good intentions, and use our resources to advance their selfish interests. Burden-bearing always carries the risk of failure.[40]

If sacrifice creates relational change, we should count our blessings and be pleasantly surprised at the by-product of what otherwise is joyful living in the imitation of Christ.

THE PHILOSOPHY OF SACRIFICE

I was a clumsy teenager, and I met my wife when we were thirteen-years-old, so I had a habit of breaking things around her parent's house. The destruction slowed down after we got older and, as I got married, enough to the point that it became a joke when I was at the in-laws. But I still felt embarrassed.

One night, however, we were making dinner for the family at my wife's parent's house, and I burned a wooden spoon on the skillet to the point that it had to be thrown out. Though we had been married for years, my wife and I were immediately mindful of the embarrassment for those many times that I broke things in that home. So my

---

40 Sittser, *Love one Another,* 142.

wife did a sacrificial, loving act. She went to her mother, holding the spoon, and said, "This got burned. Sorry." She didn't lie, but she didn't make me 'fess up to it either. It was no big deal to her mom, but what my wife said was a big deal for me.

Sacrifice can come in a variety of forms. Sometimes it can be taking the blame. I am not suggesting that you do anything dishonest. But there may come an occasion where you can, in an honest way, alleviate the blame for another person. It may cost you very little; what's a burned spoon on your record? But it may benefit the other person much, lifting a burden that seems unbearable to them but light to you.

WHEN TO SACRIFICE

I have stated repeatedly in this book that each of the nine options for relational change serves the fundamental option of instruction. Sacrifice is no exception. You sacrifice when you think it is in the other person's best interest and when you think it will be instructive. You don't sacrifice when you think it will fail to instruct or when you would otherwise be enabling someone to go on in a sinful or destructive pattern.

In the chapter on "Make a Boundary" (chapter seven), I mention the difference between a broken will and a broken spirit. The primary purpose of instruction is to break someone's sinful will, never to break their spirit. The burned spoon was not a sin; it was an accident. I did not need to learn some lesson, so I was not in need of having my will broken. My wife immediately recognized that, though my will was not an issue, my spirit was in need of care. So she aided in lifting my spirit.

It is important to make this distinction because there are times when people are tempted to sacrifice for another, but to do so would prevent them from a broken will when brokenness may be necessary.

WHY SACRIFICE

I can think of three reasons why we should sacrifice. One is that it demonstrates *solidarity* with the other person. When our oldest son first learned to drive, controlling the car must have absorbed all that his mind could handle because he forgot where he parked. He went by himself to a New Year's festival in a town with which he was unfamiliar, and parking was scarce. He had to park on a residential street a mile from where the festival was; and when he walked back to find his car, he couldn't remember the street, let alone the block! So my wife got in the car, drove to the festival, and spent a couple hours going from street to street with him looking for it.

It was tempting to let him solve his own problem, and there surely was a lesson to be learned here. But the lesson was clear enough to him without our help. Not a word needed to be said for him to appropriately learn, "Make a note of where you park." However much we didn't want to be scouring the strange neighborhood in the middle of the night, he wanted this to be happening even less. Helping him find the car was not enabling him to continue in some negative pattern; this experience cost him a great deal, even though we "rescued" him.

The purpose of coming to his assistance was to demonstrate our solidarity with him. We wanted him to learn a lesson, but we wanted to be on his side as he learned it. We don't want him ever to question whose side we are on. In every moment of instruction, we stand with him. I am convinced that he learned a lesson that night every bit as clearly as if we had not helped him, and he got the bonus of knowing we were in solidarity with him.

Any time you feel called to sacrifice, you will be giving up something you are entitled to have (otherwise, it's not a sacrifice). You may have every right in the world to get your own way, to keep your stuff, or to maintain your position. But sometimes, sacrifice expresses solidarity with the other person, and that is worth more than getting your way or keeping your stuff.

In the book *Connecting*, Larry Crabb recounts the power of sacrificing himself (which he refers to as his own death and resurrection) to create relational change. He writes:

> *I have experienced death in the presence of my wife and a few friends. They have watched the process, they have fixed nothing and exhorted nothing, but they have poured into me the hope that death precedes life, that death to self is the route to finding oneself, that crucifixion means Resurrection is coming. Because we died together, because we connected during the experience of death, we now live together. We experience fellowship in Christ, the real thing that only he can provide.*[41]

If we are simply looking for someone else to change their behavior, then sacrifice may not have a powerful effect. But if we are looking for what Crabb calls "the real thing" of fellowship, then sacrifice is absolutely essential.

The second reason we should sacrifice is to be merciful. The psalmist exclaims, "he does not treat us as our sins deserve or repay

41 Crabb, *Connecting*, 101.

us according to our iniquities" (Ps. 103:10). Many of the options for relational change in this book involve "dealing with people according to their iniquity."

I have offered ways to speak the truth when someone sins. You can appeal emotionally when they offend you. You can make a boundary, leave, or let them suffer the consequences of you "doing nothing." But how often does God deal with us according to our sin? We must admit that the majority of the time, God does not intervene. You may be thinking, "But He lets us suffer the consequences of our sin." Sometimes, but not always. God is merciful in that we could not handle knowing the true extent of our own sin, nor could we handle suffering the consequences of our sin.

Sacrifice is also an act of mercy because it can end suffering, even suffering that is self-inflicted by sin. My daughter Natasha hates to do the laundry. She has a flair for the dramatic, so she combines that skill with her hesitation to do the laundry, for a perfect performance of suffering in rebellion. The laundry becomes heavy, the pieces infinite, the time never-ending, the experience solitary, and the clothing uncooperative. Each step communicates, "Will anyone in the world take note of the injustice which my parents require?" Though the performance is simultaneously hilarious and offensive, it also indicates a need for repentance in her heart.

But one time I felt that the situation had become more than she could bear—not the laundry, but the rebellion. I knew that excusing her from the laundry would not address the rebellion in her heart. But I desperately wanted to help her both with the laundry and her rebellion. Sometimes, discipline can do that. But this time I saw that she had slipped so far into a pit of despair that discipline would only harden her heart.

So I worked side by side with her in solidarity to finish the laundry. Since she was "suffering," I suffered with her. I don't think it would work every time, nor would it be called for every time, but somehow this time I thought it was what she needed. And I was right. Her attitude about laundry subsequently improved.

I spoke at a high school youth group retreat, where the kids were inordinately rowdy. That's partly because the youth pastor had them arrange all the mattresses in the living room of the rented house so that the guys could wrestle. Eventually, the leaders went to sleep, but the young men continued wrestling.

In the morning, Tim, the youth pastor, discovered that the guys wrestled so vigorously that the ceiling fan in the room below had fallen to the ground. Tim asked all the guys to gather, and he asked who continued wrestling after the adults went to sleep. No one would 'fess up.

The answer to this question was important, partly because it would give the guys a chance to repent. But the damage to the ceiling fan also had to be fixed, and someone would have to pay. Tim knew it was wise to only demand things over which he had control, and he could not control whether he got a confession from these guys. Yet he wanted them to see that if they did not take responsibility, someone else would have to pay.

So after sufficient time of asking the youth to confess and to pitch in for the repairs, he took out $50 from his wallet, and said, "The price must be paid by someone. I will pay the price." His sacrifice was intentional, joyful, and freely given. At the time, Tim believed that sacrifice was in the best interest of the kids he was instructing. It was a demonstration of the vicarious sacrifice that Christ offered for us. Everyone in the room was moved by this picture of the Kingdom of God.

Our children know (or at least they should by now) that we like them to take out a new box of toys only after they have put the previous ones away. We still have to reiterate this expectation on the weekends, when they have more time to put their full heart, mind, and strength into giving all their toys attention. Once we see the Legos, the dress-up clothes, and the skyscraper marble set, we know it's time for a stern warning: "You may not get any more toys out, and you will have to clean all of these up."

When our daughter Leah was four years old, she got herself in way over her head. When it came time to clean up, she was truly terrified at the sight she had created (as were we). We told her in advance not to make such a mess; we reminded her; and we warned her that she was going to have a lot of work to do. But when my wife and I saw the full extent of the mess, we realized that this burden may be unbearable. How did we respond? The decision-making criterion I have offered in this book is, "What is in the best interest of the other person?" And with regard to parenting, I am specifically asking, "What will be most instructional?"

To answer this question, when my wife and I observed Leah's disaster of the play room, we were looking for a particular response. We wanted to see that she had a broken will, but not a broken spirit. In other words, we wanted to see that she was repentant. We had no interest in punishing her or causing her to suffer the consequences any further than she needed to reach repentance. The moment we told her to clean her room, her repentance was obvious. The look on her face revealed grief, remorse, and fear. Once she obeyed and began to start cleaning, my wife and I began to help.

I was reminded of 2 Corinthians 2:5-11, where Paul instructed the Corinthians how to deal with a repentant man in their congregation. In his first letter, he told the church to expel him from their midst so that he would repent. But in the second letter, Paul said they should welcome the repentant man back, "so that he will not be overwhelmed by excessive sorrow" (v. 7). In our relationships with others, especially as parents, we do not need to elicit excessive sorrow. We pray that others, and ourselves, will incur only the exact amount of grief necessary to keep us in a right relationship with God.

The third reason we should sacrifice is to be a demonstration of Christ. I could have said "to imitate Christ," but our act of sacrifice is more than an example; it is an incarnation. We do more than represent Christ when we sacrifice; we actually serve as His body.

Jesus epitomized sacrifice. Sacrifice was the precise reason that God took on flesh. Undoubtedly, the sacrifice was difficult, for Jesus prayed three times that the Father would "remove this cup from me" (Lk. 22:42). Yet sacrifice was freely given and joyfully offered. We read, "Yet it was the LORD'S will to crush him . . . " (Isa. 53:10).

We read in the Old Testament that Christ intended to offer Himself as a sacrifice long before He came to earth. Isaiah writes, "He was oppressed and afflicted, yet he did not open his mouth; he was led like a lamb to the slaughter, and as a sheep before its shearers is silent, so he did not open his mouth" (Isa. 53:7).

Throughout the New Testament, Christ's followers are encouraged to imitate His attitude of sacrifice. Peter reminds us, "When they hurled their insults at him, he did not retaliate; when he suffered, he made no threats. Instead, he entrusted himself to him who judges justly" (1 Pet. 2:23).

TYPES OF SACRIFICE

There are a variety of ways that you may feel called to sacrifice as an act of love or mercy. You may sense that this sacrifice is for the benefit of other people or for your relationship with them. These occasions include:

- Paying a debt. A friend may owe a debt to you that is overwhelming, and perhaps even impossible. You may sense that their spirit is right with you, and they are grieved or repentant (if applicable). You may absolve the debt as an intentional gift of sacrifice.
- Taking a loss. My best friend and I own several pieces of equipment together. Every time he uses the paint sprayer, I have to replace the tip, strainer, and handle. And every time he takes out the wave runner, I have to replace a mirror, bilge pump, dust cover, battery, etc. Our relationship is not worth making an issue of these costs. I replace these things as an "offering to the LORD, a pleasing aroma, a[n] . . . offering presented to the LORD" (Exod. 29:18). So I just determined that whenever he used the paint sprayer, it was going to cost me an extra $30. I remembered Paul's words, "Why not rather be wronged?" (1 Cor. 6:7). The best answer I could come up with was, "Because it costs me $30." I understand that your friend could cost you $300, or $3000, and then we would have to come up with a dollar amount at which it is no longer

feasible to "be wronged." Such a dollar amount does not exist. Sacrifice will not always be the right or best option. But it is sometimes, and you will have to let the Holy Spirit help you determine when.

- Doing the work. Every group has a longsuffering servant who is willing to do the work for others. If you can be such a person, and do it with sincere joy, then you will experience a beautiful act of sacrifice.

- Taking the blame. We often do everything we can to prevent taking blame. One of the first skills toddlers learn is to respond to the question, "Did you . . . " with "No!" But taking the blame can be a beautiful way to sacrifice, and often, taking the blame costs you nothing.

I have suggested that sacrifice is a means of relational change, and it is. But Larry Crabb cautions:

> It is not the job of community to change people. Only the Spirit can do that . . . We may sometimes rebuke and provide disruptive feedback (we must always do it reluctantly), but we must never insist that our disruption accomplish a deep spiritual work. We must never demand a response to our intervention, but rather we should pray for one. When we do require that our involvement generate an effect, we usurp the Holy Spirit's role and usually find ourselves in the middle of a power struggle.[42]

The sacrifice that Jesus exemplified was silent, not demanding. Jesus sacrificed, and in doing so, the Holy Spirit moved in some people's hearts to respond and repent. Others did not. In either case, Jesus entrusted "Himself to Him who judges justly" (1 Pet. 2:23).

---

42 Crabb, *Connecting*, 131.

CHAPTER 5

DO NOTHING

SOMETIMES, DOING NOTHING CREATES RELATIONAL change. In the case of Marie's dysfunctional relationship with her mother and sister, doing nothing is indeed a legitimate strategy. She could do nothing out of a determination to let the problem worsen until it becomes obvious to her mother and sister. There is a risk here, of course, because it may be that those she lives with will never see the bathroom as a crisis. Or, even if there is some theoretical level of disgust in the bathroom that would alarm her sister and mother, that point is clearly well beyond Marie's comfort level, so she is likely to buckle from her resolve to wait for others to fix the problem.

On the other hand, she could do nothing out of a strong, peaceful decision to not let the messiness of the bathroom bother her. This is certainly difficult, but not impossible. I am not saying that she will have a positive or neutral emotional response to the bathroom, but she can make a conscious decision to just accept the reality that this is the way things are. Living with her mother and sister means having a dirty bathroom.

When you continually try to change things that are outside of your control, there is great serenity in accepting the fact that you cannot do it. Resign from the task because it is not in your job description. But don't resign in anger, as if the people around you are a lost cause. Instead, resign in peace because you realize that this is just the way life is.

We are all tempted to *do* too much or to do the wrong things. Especially when we are trapped, we want to act. But sometimes, we end up addressing the wrong issue.

One time, our family was in Yellowstone National Park, and we saw a grizzly bear. We pulled over at a safe distance to take a photo, but we did want to get outside for a clearer shot. Before my wife got out of our car to take a picture of a grizzly bear, however, she put on bug spray. We all laughed hysterically at the irony. Bug spray is not going to protect you from a grizzly! The threat of mosquito bites may have been more imminent and likely than any other danger, but the very act of protecting herself from mosquitoes in the face of a grizzly was hilarious.

When you feel trapped, you will be tempted to act. In this compulsion, you will likely address the wrong issues. For that reason, it's advisable once in a while to do nothing, wait, think, and see.

DEFINITION OF "DOING NOTHING"

"The intentional decisions to let someone else fail or succeed without your intervention."

You may be wondering what is the difference between sacrifice and "doing nothing." These two concepts are very similar. Presumably, if you "do nothing," the other person is going to get their way, and you will not get yours (thus, you have sacrificed something). But I think there is a key difference, depending on who is more affected by the decision.

When you sacrifice, you are more affected by the decision. When you "do nothing," the other person is more affected. There are actually many areas of conflict where "doing nothing" is a viable option, and it will ultimately affect the other person far more than it affects you. This can be very instructive, and, as I stated in chapter one, communicating truth is the ultimate goal of all nine options. You can communicate truth by doing nothing.

When we speak of sacrifice, we always imply a personal cost. When we choose to sacrifice, often the other alternative is to confront. For instance, if my son says something rude to me, I can either confront him, or I can overlook this particular instance (within a greater context of teaching him) as an intentional extension of grace.

But often when we "do nothing," the other alternative is called "enabling." For instance, if a good friend has a gambling problem and asks me to help cover his rent, I could do one of the following:

- Help him out as an act of grace,
- Confront him or teach him the truth and consequences of his actions, or
- Do nothing (don't help him out).

Helping this friend with the rent may very well be the most loving action. It may be the easiest, if you find it unbearable to have someone angry with you. But the criterion offered in this book is, "What is in the best interest of the other person?" On occasion, it may be that giving financial help is in the other person's interest. Failure to attain that help could cause him to be overcome with grief and despair or may result in a financial quagmire from which he is unlikely ever to recover.

But when people have addictive behaviors, the time quickly comes when helping them is no longer in their best interest. It may be an act of grace to help the first time my friend asks for help to get him out of a gambling debt, but it is cruel to help him the tenth time. That's because I would no longer be (back to option 1) telling him the truth and consequences. If I continue to help, I create a false sense of assurance that his actions have no consequences.

It is cruel to let people live under this illusion. It is dishonest because, eventually, they will reap what they have sown. Doing nothing can allow someone to experience the consequences of their sin sooner and, thereby, mercifully rescue them sooner. In this sense, doing nothing is an agent of relational change.

IGNORING: THE NEGATIVE COUSIN OF "DOING NOTHING"

The negative cousin of "doing nothing" is to ignore or "blow people off." Tom, an elderly man in our church, has a mantra that seems well-meaning but, upon second thought, strikes some as quite offensive. He says, "You can't offend me. Nothing can offend me. I only care what Christ thinks."

At first hearing, this maxim is reassuring. It sounds as if he is a friend toward all and will accept others unconditionally. But as the line sinks in, I find myself thinking, "Why can't I offend him? What if I tried really hard? Is it because he thinks so little of my opinion that he can disregard it? Has he decided to take everything I say with a grain of salt? Is he just blowing me off?"

When others try to engage us emotionally and we "do nothing," we might be sending the signal that we do not value the relationship enough to dignify them with a response. So when I say, "Do nothing," I do not mean to blow people off. Value others enough to respond to them.

Let's look back to my criterion of how to choose among the nine positive options. We don't decide to "do nothing" simply because we feel like doing nothing. Instead, we "do nothing" when we are convinced that it is in the other person's best interest. We are convinced that this is how Christ would act and the option that will most help in their discipleship. I can think of a few instances in the Bible where "doing nothing" is best for the other person.

WHAT DOING NOTHING LOOKS LIKE IN THE BIBLE

The church in Corinth tolerated a sexually immoral man. The Apostle Paul says that he was sleeping with his stepmother, and the church was bragging about their progressive attitude of tolerance. Shockingly, Paul admonished the Corinthians to "hand this man over to Satan" (1 Cor. 5:5). In other words, he encouraged them to have nothing to do with a person who calls himself a Christian but refuses to repent of sin, even when he is confronted with it. They were to refuse to fellowship with a person who continues to live in sin.

The purpose here, however, was to win him back. Paul says that turning the man away is the only way they could possibly give him a chance to be saved. God is too merciful to allow us to be confused about whom we serve. He will not allow us to convince ourselves that we are Christians who get away with habitual, unrepentant sin. It would be cruel of God to allow us to have false security. The church is expected to reflect God's mercy in this way. We are also to help people see the God that they truly serve.

Evidently, Paul's plan for the Corinthians worked. He wrote in his second letter that the man who repented should be reinstated by the church. His repentance was enough. In fact, Paul said he did not want the precious brother to be "overcome with excessive sorrow" (2 Cor. 2:7). How did it work? The church sent a clear message that he had to choose whom he would serve. They graciously forced him to choose which life he would lead, rather than allow him to have the false impression that he could have a divided heart.

When Jesus sent out His disciples on a mission, He gave them instruction for their travel. Jesus told them, "And if any place will not welcome you or listen to you, leave that place and shake the dust off your feet as a testimony against them" (Mk. 6:11). Jesus Himself experienced this rejection and acted accordingly.

We read that He could not do miracles in His hometown or surrounding villages because they did not believe (Mk 6:5). And He was driven out of other towns. But in all of this, Jesus did not protest. He knew that the truth of the Gospel would speak for itself. It did not need force, continued pleading, or stronger delivery. He offered the truth and let it do its job. That job, according to Jesus, is to "prove the world to be in the wrong about sin and righteousness and judgment" (Jn. 16:8).

Jesus quoted Isaiah, who said, "Though seeing, they do not see; though hearing, they do not hear or understand" (Matt. 13:13). Is this a hateful or a loving thing to say about someone? Your heart could be in either place when you say it. I trust that Jesus uttered it out of love, albeit a stern, loving warning. Nevertheless, it is an utterance of resignation. But such resignation is loving to both parties involved.

It is best for you to accept the things you cannot change, lest you drive yourself crazy. And it is loving to others to accept them for who they are. Jesus offered the option of "doing nothing" when He said, "Do not throw your pearls to pigs" (Matt. 7:6). In other words, we are not to continue offering truth to someone who will not listen.

Not all expressions of "doing nothing" have to be resigning or weighty ones as I just described. On the opposite side of the spectrum, sometimes we may choose to "do nothing" because the issue really is not a big deal or because the other person is about to change.

In 2 Samuel 16, King David shocked his entourage when he "did nothing." The king was proceeding through the streets when he was confronted on the roadside by an eccentric character named Shimei. The man yelled curses at the king: "Get out, get out, you murderer, you scoundrel!" (2 Sam. 16:7).

The witnesses expected the king to lop his head off. When the king failed to react, they offered to do the job. But David said, "Let him curse, for the LORD has told him to. It may be that the LORD will look upon my misery and restore to me his covenant blessing instead of his curse today" (2 Sam. 16:11-12). King David was content not to address the situation, trusting in the sovereignty of God.

All this is to say that doing nothing is a real option. It is not just the status quo because you are making a conscious decision to do nothing, out of your strength, benevolence (because you believe it is best for the other person at this time), and faith (because you believe God is more capable to change things than you are).

Doing nothing can be frightening. The only way we can justify employing this skill of relational change is to take confidence in the sovereignty of God. If there is no God, then we have need to worry about "doing nothing." Without the presence, power, or concern of God, everything is up to us. If the relationship is going to change, you better do something. But with the confidence that God is present, in control, and deeply concerned, we can take comfort that, even when we do nothing, God is fully engaged and active. God continues to work on people's hearts, speak to their minds, and supervene over the universe while you do nothing. With God in control, we need not fear when we do nothing as an act of obedience and faith.

Some people may object that doing nothing allows us to shirk our responsibility of keeping people accountable and confronting them about their sin. But not every sin demands a confrontation. After all, that is not how God treats us. We read in the Psalms, "He does not treat us as our sins deserve or repay us according to our iniquities" (Ps. 103:10). If God sees fit not to confront us on every sin, then surely we can graciously keep silent sometimes too.

WHAT DOING NOTHING LOOKS LIKE IN MARRIAGE

My wife and I found our first year of marriage to be the most difficult. In the first couple months, I identified for her several of the things that she needed to change. That didn't go well, so then I needed to add one more thing to the list—"more receptive to criticism."

One of my concerns was that I thought she was "clingy." I thought, "I don't want to deal with this for 50 years." A wise friend said to me, "Could you deal with it for one year, if you knew that a year later the situation would improve?" *Sure*, I thought.

Knowing that I could wait a year to deal with it took the pressure off for the day. Good relationships can handle correction and the stress of confrontation, but even the best relationships can't handle it every day. There are limits to the amount of stress a relationship can handle.

In our first year of marriage, we needed to find fewer occasions for confrontation and to choose our battles more wisely. It occurred to me that what I perceived as my wife's "clinginess" was not something that needed immediate attention—or even attention this year. In fact, I realized that we had 50 years to work on it, and doing so would be the joy of participating in God's lifelong work of sanctifying us. Throughout that first year, I learned the peaceful, liberating act of "doing nothing."

Gottman makes a startling admission to couples who seek counseling:

> Most marital arguments cannot be resolved. Couples spend year after year trying to change each other's minds—but it can't be done. This is because most of their disagreements are rooted in fundamental differences of lifestyle, personality, or values. By fighting over these differences, all they succeed in doing is wasting their time and harming their marriage.[43]

---

43 Gottman, *The Seven Principles for Making Marriage Work*, 23-24.

At first, this admission seems like bad business. If conflict can't be resolved, why go to counseling? I shared this news with couples and saw the look of disappointment or horror on their faces. Then I second-guessed whether I should break this news to them. Isn't my job as a counselor to instill hope? And wouldn't it be better for business to promise success?

But Gottman's admission is actually quite hope-inspiring. What he is saying is that the argument cannot be resolved in the sense that two people who disagree will come to agree. Nor should we expect this of others. To expect that an argument can be resolved by agreement is essentially saying, "If you are smart, you will see it my way."

If you expect people to agree with you, then you imply that this will be accomplished by persuasion, genius, or force. But your friend, co-worker, child, or spouse is intelligent and has a valid perspective. Agreement is not the resolution you need or are looking for. What you need from each other is love, acceptance, sacrifice, empathy, and repentance. If that is the definition of resolution, then conflict can be resolved.

One of the foundational principles of Gottman's *Relationship Cure* is, "Despite what many therapists will tell you, you don't have to resolve your major marital conflicts for your marriage to thrive."[44] When I was a professional counselor, I made the initial mistake of passing this trade secret on to a couple during the first session.

I cited Gottman, "Very few conflicts can be resolved. The best we can hope for is repair." As soon as the words left my mouth, I knew I would never see them again and that I was embarking on a poor

---

44 Gottman, *The Seven Principles for Making Marriage Work*, 131.

business model. People come to counseling to get their problems resolved. If that can't be done, then what are they spending their time and money on?

Well, despite the poor business model, Gottman is still right. If you believe watching baseball is a waste of time, and your husband thinks it's a vital use of time, you are not going to resolve this conflict. You can cope, compromise, adjust, or figure out a way to deal with the conflict. And if you sin against each other, you can repair and forgive. In light of that reality, which extends to all relationships, we must brace ourselves for a whole lot of "doing nothing." Once we accept that the goal is repair, rather than resolution, we recognize that many of our conflicts are just not worth having.

WHAT DOING NOTHING LOOKS LIKE IN PARENTING

One time I asked my son, Sonny, to pick up some toys that were on the floor, and he said, "See, it's not hard. You just bend over and pick it up." Obviously, this was very disrespectful. But I was immediately brought back to my own childhood when I remembered doing the exact same thing. I responded, "I said that to my dad once. Once." And we both laughed.

Not every act of disrespect requires a response. Certainly God doesn't cause us to incur a consequence for every sin. If disrespect is continuous or if a child is unrepentant, then it is the parent's responsibility to shepherd the heart. But if I get the sense that my son is generally respectful and is repentant, I don't need to confront him every time. Sometimes we can sense repentance even if there is no confrontation or apology.

WHAT DOING NOTHING LOOKS
LIKE IN FRIENDSHIP

I had breakfast with a group of men who were frustrated with their pastor. They vented for an hour about various reasons they had lost respect for him. Many of these frustrations included things they had talked to the pastor about repeatedly. Evidently, the pastor had acknowledged these shortcomings, apologized, and promised to do better. These men were weary of the apologies and promises and were hoping for a change—whether that meant a new pastor for the church or a new church for them.

Something occurred to me as they were speaking that may have been obvious to an outsider but to which they were blind. I said, "Maybe your pastor is operating at his full capacity. Maybe what you see is all you are ever going to get. You are frustrated because you think he should be doing better, but maybe he has reached his full potential."

If this were the case, then these men might still be justified in wishing for a new pastor, but their frustration would be misguided. Their frustration was expressed in moral terms, as if the pastor was doing something wrong, unethical, or sinful. While a lack of capacity in another person may be irritating, it is not their fault. If I was right in my assessment that this pastor was operating at his capacity, then the prospect of change is very slim. And whenever we find ourselves demanding change when the prospect is slim, we have a recipe for frustration.

This group of men could petition their church for a new pastor, but beyond that, there is very little they can do. Their other option is to "do nothing." They could consciously determine to accept the fact that their pastor has reached his capacity, and this is the pastor they get. This is the work they will expect from him. Most of the men in the group heeded my advice to stop expecting him to change beyond his current capacity, and the change was immediately obvious (it was positive and a breath of fresh air).

One of the men in this group went to the pastor and said, "Pastor Dean, I hereby resign from trying to change you." Now, the pastor could have interpreted that statement in two opposite ways. He could have heard, "I give up trying to change you because you are incorrigible, stubborn, and worthless." Or he could have heard, "I give up trying to change you because it is not my place, nor is it possible for anyone to change another." Fortunately, the pastor heard the latter, the way that it was offered.

"How did it feel when you resigned from trying to change the pastor, Scott?" I asked. He said, "It was one of the most liberating things I've ever done."

I have a friend who is in the midst of a major home remodel. The contractor, Brad, is also a mutual friend of ours. The home owner, Jim, was telling me how he is not satisfied with all that Brad is doing.

Jim said, "I can't *not* call him out on it. I have to tell him the way I see it."

Where do we get the idea about what we "can't not do" or what we "have to do"? The interesting thing to me about these phrases is that for every person who says, "I can't not call him out on it," there is another person out there who equally feels, "I probably shouldn't say anything about it."

Both choices are entirely realistic. Every day, people choose actions and words that are on opposite sides of the spectrum, and these choices don't even feel like "choices." They feel entirely natural, even compulsory. Our inclination becomes our self-evident "must."

Every time you've had a bad day, someone else woke up in the same circumstances and determined that they were going to have a good day. I'll be kind and say the opposite. Every time you had a good day, someone else in the same circumstances woke up and determined to have a bad day.

Every Saturday morning, my mother works in the church kitchen with a volunteer crew that cooks breakfast for about eighty homeless guests. One of the cooks, George, is contentious. I've experienced his grumbling a few times, and others have told me their own stories. But every week, my mother worked with this man, and I never heard her complain. I asked her about George's bickering, and she didn't seem particularly bothered. That bothered me. I wrestled with how she could not be bothered. It seemed like a puzzle that had to be solved. So I came up with only two possibilities:

- Maybe she is also contentious, so she approves of this type of behavior and, therefore, isn't bothered.
- Maybe she is oblivious, due to stupidity or selective blindness.

In other words, one way or another, she is deficient for not being bothered by George. The only reasons not to be angry with him are stupidity or sin. It is the morally right thing to be irritated with George. But as I talked further with her, I realized that she was not blind to George's contentiousness; she just wasn't angry about it. And I know her well enough to know she is not contentious herself, nor is she stupid. Evidently, there was a third explanation for her lack of moral indignation:

- She is gracious.

She sees George's sin but loves him despite of it. She recognizes that George's whole personality and his total value cannot be determined solely by one sinful behavior. I realized that I was the one who was deficient. All of the cooks on the kitchen crew found reasons to love this man, whom I had a hard time loving. They had a level of grace which I lacked. When I realized that I was the person who was lacking, I was truly humbled. A richer life awaited me, with more joy, and a larger capacity from which to serve as a conduit of God's love. I saw in this group the ministry of graciously "doing nothing."

CHAPTER 6

LEAVE

THERE IS AN OPTION FOR relational change that is more drastic than the previous two chapters, which concentrated on "sacrificing" or "doing nothing." One option that Marie has in her relationship with her mother and sister is to leave. Marie can move elsewhere out of her home with her mom. To leave is not to sever the relationship permanently. In fact, sometimes the only way to preserve a relationship is by temporary separation.

DEFINITION OF LEAVE

"The intentional decision temporarily to separate because it is in the other person's best interest."

STORMING OUT: THE NEGATIVE COUSIN OF "LEAVING"

The "negative cousin" of leaving is storming out. When you storm out of a room, you act impulsively. You never think to yourself in advance, "I think I will storm out now." Storming out is never a selfless act with the other person's best interest in mind. It's not as if you say, "It looks like storming out is the most loving option and the best way to reflect God's character to you." But it is possible to leave someone and do it with their best interest in mind. You can leave intentionally and with forethought.

Some spouses get in the car and drive off. Some hang up the phone abruptly. Others slam the door. One of my wife's biggest fears used to be that I would leave the room in the middle of an argument. She felt terribly abandoned. To some extent, she even felt irrationally abandoned, in the sense that this act brings to memory previous times in her life when she felt abandoned. But in the midst of conflict, I have felt the strong urge to flee, and I've done it impulsively.

WHERE WE SEE LEAVING IN THE BIBLE

We read in Ezekiel 10:4 that the glory of the Lord filled the temple and consumed the altar. But tragically, the prophet also saw the glory of the Lord leave. When this happened, the nation of Israel incurred tragic consequences. Ezekiel foresaw (and it came to pass) that the nation would be taken captive by Babylon. One might see here that God has conditional love and that He is capricious.

But on the contrary, the author of Hebrews tells us that God disciplines those whom He loves. Since we are His children, He honors us with discipline. If we were not His children (illegitimate, as the author of Hebrews says), then God would just see us as a "lost cause." But the fact that He disciplines us proves He hasn't given up on us.

The Babylonian captivity of Israel was understood by the prophets as a temporary abandonment by God with the purpose of discipline and restoration. The prophets knew it would last about 70 years, and 1 Chronicles states that the reason for this was to make up for the 70 Sabbath years that the Israelites had failed to observe according to the Law during the previous 420 years.

Moses decreed that the land should lay fallow (unfarmed) every seven years in order to give the land rest. Allowing the land to go unfarmed is an act of faith, however. It demands that the people trust there will be enough to eat. Apparently they didn't have the faith to keep this part of the Law, so they failed to give the land its rest. But this was not the main reason that God allowed the nation to be taken captive.

Their primary sin was idolatry. Throughout the entire time that the people enjoyed the kingdom established by David, which lasted about 400 years, the people continued to offer sacrifices to foreign gods. The Lord gave them repeated opportunities to repent. Some kings destroyed these idols (or high places), where sacrifices were offered to other gods. But these reforms were short-lived because monotheism did not capture the hearts of the people.

God equated idolatry to prostitution, and it was to remedy this unfaithfulness that God saw fit to withdraw His protection from the people. God's decision was selfless and had His people's best interest in mind. In order to allure His people back to Himself, He was left with the heart-wrenching decision to "leave."

The Babylonian captivity was devastating to Israel. The temple was destroyed, as was the city of Jerusalem and its walls. What's more tragic is their religious practice almost completely disappeared from memory. Nobody read the Law during that time. It was later rediscovered by Ezra. And as he read it to the people, they wept because they had not realized how much they had failed to do. The temple was rebuilt, as was the city of Jerusalem. And when the temple returned, so did the glory of the Lord.

Could leaving ever be loving? If Jesus condoned the action of leaving, then I trust that it can be loving. When Jesus sent out the 72 missionaries, He gave them instructions: "If anyone will not welcome you or receive your words, leave that home or town and shake the dust off your feet" (Matt. 10:14). This is a surprisingly harsh reaction from the mouth of Jesus, but it illustrates that leaving can be loving.

Why did Jesus want His disciples to leave towns that rejected them? So as not to waste their time? Solely to make them more effective somewhere else? To prevent them from being discouraged or angry? To keep them from getting killed?

None of these reasons really touches on the absolute quality of the goodness of God. Jesus would only have commanded that the disciples leave unresponsive towns if it was *good* to do so. My unwavering belief in the unconditional love and sacrificial character of God compels me to believe that leaving was in these towns' best interest.

Paul explains this concept of leaving as "handing them over" (1 Cor. 5:5, 1 Tim. 1:20). Long ago, Alcoholics Anonymous figured out that the most loving thing friends of problem drinkers can do is "give them over." As long as there is an enabling friend, an alcoholic may be able to successfully straddle two worlds—one with family and job and the other with alcohol. But once his enabling friends "give him over," he learns who he serves. He no longer can fool himself into thinking that things are OK.

Paul and Barnabas also evidently came to the point where they believed that "leaving" was the best option for dealing with a conflict between themselves, which the Bible refers to as a "sharp disagreement" (Acts 15:36-40).

The Bible explains how it could be helpful with the concept of "hardness of heart." Jesus was so gracious that He would not allow certain towns to live under the false impression that they were OK with God. This would be cruel. In Mark 6:5-6, we read that Jesus briefly visited His hometown of Nazareth, but His ministry was truncated because He, "Could not do miracles there . . . [and] He was amazed at their lack of faith."

Was it loving for Him to leave? Shouldn't He have stayed in the town until He was able to convince many, if not a few, people to believe? Our assumption that staying is better seems to make sense, but in some cases, it is clearly not working. If it isn't working, doesn't trying harder mean trying something else? What is to say that leaving won't have a more persuasive effect than staying?

WHAT LEAVING LOOKS LIKE IN MARRIAGE

Is it possible to leave, hang up, or drive off, but to do it with self-control? And can it be done selflessly? I think it can be done. An argument on the phone may escalate to the point that it seems like the wisest option is to hang up. But this needs to be done in such a way that it doesn't make the other person feel abandoned or like you are "storming out."

Rick had a habit of hanging up on the phone with Katie. To some extent, this was wise because when he didn't hang up, he usually ended up saying hurtful things that he regretted later. I suggested to Rick that if he truly felt that this was the best option for the relationship, he should first say calmly and clearly to his wife, "I'm going to hang up now. I will call you back in 30 minutes. I love you." This is a form of "leaving" that exercises self-control and expresses commitment to the relationship.

My wife and I have taken an interest in the Discovery Channel show, *Intervention*. The show features people with drug or alcohol addictions whose family members intervene in order to show their loved one how much they care. Ironically, I think the show could equally be called, The Enablers. It is striking how in each episode, it is clear that the family members who love the addict the most are also making the addiction possible.

Behind every person with an addiction is an enabler. This is true whether the addict is a spouse, parent, child, or even homeless. People with addictions are often so dysfunctional that they cannot sustain their addiction without help. They need shelter, money, and access to their substance. Also ironic, therefore, is that the most loving thing loved ones can do is separate in order to end the enabling. Ideally, in the case of addiction, this means that the addict goes to a treatment center. The radical step of requiring the addict to undergo treatment is a selfless form of "leaving." Of course, the addict may choose not to go. In this case, the enablers must determine that they will be the ones to leave.

"Leaving" can be a strategy for relational change. But it is also important for you. Sometimes, it is not only the most effective thing to do, but it is also the right thing to do. Dr. Dobson's book, *Love Must Be Tough*, explains: "Respect, the critical ingredient in human affairs, is generated by quiet dignity, self-confidence, and common courtesy. It is assassinated by hand wringing, groveling in the dirt, and pleas for mercy."[45] Often the self-resect that Dobson advocates in the book re-

---

45 Dobson, *Love Must Be Tough*, 75.

quires leaving. But it is always purposeful leaving with an intention to save, rather than destroy, the relationship.

Dobson makes a case for loving, redemptive, temporary separation in troubled marriages. Especially in the cases of substance abuse or physical abuse, all other efforts to effect change may fail. Unfortunately, when this happens, many spouses call it quits. They say they've tried everything, and nothing changed, so now all they can do is leave. Dobson argues that leaving can be part of the strategy for relational change, not for relational dissolution. But in order for separation to have this positive effect, several rules must be followed:

- The separation must be intentional (not flippant or impulsive).

- The separation must be for the purpose of reunification (not testing the waters or taking a "wait and see approach").

- The separation must be purposeful. You tell your partner what you would like to see happen and when.

- The separation must have a clearly defined time frame. You explain that you will come back together when certain benchmarks have been achieved.

- The separation must be moderated. You don't get to come up with an arbitrary laundry list of things for the other person to do. Get a counselor, pastor, or friend to moderate this list of benchmarks and the time frame.

The criterion of decision-making I have repeated in this book is that we ask, "What is in the other person's best interest?" Sometimes leaving is in the other person's best interest. A blessing about healthy relationships is that often what is in the other person's best interest is also in our best interest. Sometimes, leaving is in your best interest.

But there may be reasons to leave, teach, appeal, etc., even without the other person's interest being your driving concern. For instance, Dobson relates a letter from a woman who discovered that her husband was unfaithful:

> Finally, the Lord directed me to a wise counselor who sat and listened to my story. I told him of my great guilt for the role I played in our problems and how terrible I felt. I'll never forget his reply.
>
> He told me not to take the blame for my husband's affair, and that nothing I had done could justify his infidelity. He advised me to stand up and be firm with him, even though it would be difficult. It was, he said, the only way to save our marriage. We agreed that divorce was not the answer, even though I had scriptural grounds to leave him. I decided to pay the price to confront my husband.
>
> A few months later the crisis came. I gave Milan an ultimatum—either go with the other woman or stay with me. He could not have both of us any longer. I put my hands on his shoulder and looked him straight in the eye and said, "You know you are to blame for what has happened to us. You committed adultery, I didn't." I told him if he loved the other woman more than me, then he should leave. I would accept it. I reminded him that he had a soul and would someday answer to God. Milan not only broke off the affair, but he later thanked me for having the courage to stick it out with him through this difficult time. It was not easy but we worked it out and our family survived.[46]

---

46 Dobson, *Love Must be Tough*, 75.

Dobson makes the argument that relationships involving substance abuse or infidelity will almost never experience change unless one person has the self-respect and strength to allow the other to experience consequences. Purposeful leaving can communicate calm confidence that the other person has a problem which simply must change; there is no other option.

WHAT LEAVING LOOKS LIKE IN PARENTING

Susan, like many other parents, is the mother of "boomerang kids" (adult children you throw out but then come back). She came to me asking for advice about how to deal with her grown daughter, who lives with her. Her daughter, Jessica, watches cartoons while wearing her sweatpants and eating Cheerios on the couch in the afternoons. It is absolutely clear that Susan loves her daughter and even enjoys her company at home. But she knows that Jessica is not on a path to maturity. She is not looking for work or progressing in school, so there is little indication that her life will be different 10 years from now.

Susan has a dilemma: She wants her daughter to mature, but she also wants her to feel loved. And she knows that helping Jessica grow up probably means giving her an ultimatum—to find some worthwhile way to occupy her time or move out. Susan is not primarily responsible for her daughter's actions; Jessica is. But she has made it easy for her to live in her current lifestyle. She is enabling Jessica to develop self-defeating behavior.

When Susan considers giving her such an ultimatum, she is flooded with many of her own objections and questions. She thinks, "Jessica will probably throw a fit and be mad at me, or she'll suffer if I kick her out because she won't have anywhere to go, and I'll feel terrible." These concerns are driven by the desire to be liked. But equally, we are often driven by the desire to have power. So she expressed other concerns: "How am I going to make her get a job?" "What if she doesn't do what I say?"

One of the key issues that Susan has to deal with is boundaries. As an enabler, she has allowed her daughter to maintain a self-defeating lifestyle. She was so afraid of causing pain in someone else's life that she was unable to say "no" to her daughter without feeling guilty. She feared that Jessica would lash out in anger if she kicked her out of the home or if she refused to provide for her. But even more keenly, she felt miserable about causing any unnecessary suffering for her daughter. As long as it was within her power to alleviate some pain for her, she would do it. So as long as her daughter needed a place to stay, and she could provide it, she would oblige.

But is Susan's enabling behavior loving? She came to me because she was conflicted and knew there was something wrong with what she was doing. She knew that the Bible says, "Whoever spares the rod hates their children, but the one who loves their children is careful to discipline them" (Prov. 13:24). Though her daughter was certainly beyond the age of spanking, she knew that, even as an adult, Jessica needed some discipline, and she was failing to provide it.

So here is how Susan answered those questions above:

- "I am an agent of God in discipling my children."
- "My role is to be the image of Christ in their lives."
- "I have been used to enable my daughter, but I will now be used by God to mature her."

Henry Cloud and John Townsend explain the importance of establishing boundaries—not only for our own protection, but out of love for others. First, they explain what a boundary is. "Boundaries are anything that helps to differentiate you from someone else, or shows where you begin and end."[47] Some people think that establishing a boundary is selfish and unloving, but Cloud and Townsend are convinced that boundaries improve and save relationships. They ask: "How many marriages could have been saved if one spouse had followed through with the threat of 'if you don't stop drinking (or coming home at midnight, or hitting me or yelling at the kids), I will leave until you get some treatment!'"[48]

If Susan, the enabling mother above, establishes boundaries with her "kidult" (children old enough to be adults but still acting like kids) daughter, she increases the likelihood of Jessica's success and of the success of their relationship. But when I mentioned this to her, she was unsure. She asked the same question that Cloud and Townsend address, "Don't boundaries turn us from other-centeredness to self-centeredness? The answer is no. *Appropriate boundaries actually increase our ability to care about others.*"[49] That's because caring for others means doing what is in their best interest. And drawing a boundary for someone may be the most caring thing you can do.

Not surprisingly, Susan discovered that not only did she enable her daughter to have self-defeating behavior, but she also had an enabling relationship with her husband, Glen. She rarely expressed disagreement with her husband and chose to comply with his demands for how to spend money, where to go on vacation, how to spend their

47 Cloud and Townsend, *Boundaries*, 33.
48 Cloud and Townsend, *Boundaries*, 38.
49 Cloud and Townsend, *Boundaries*, 103.

leisure time, and even what job she should have. Coming to grips with how she had been used to enable meant that she had to ask: "How will God use me in this relationship?" "What is the purpose of this relationship?"

Susan's answer was, "I am one of God's instruments in discipling my husband. God can use me to help him learn cooperation." For Susan to enable her husband's controlling behavior means that she is missing an important way for her to be used by God. God is always at work discipling His children and fashioning them into His image. Susan is one of God's children, and she has a role to play in God's work. Long before Susan came into her husband's life, God was at work chipping away at Glen's controlling disposition. It is not Susan's job to be the first voice, or the only voice, that reveals Glen's propensity to be over-bearing. God has already been speaking to him about this, through the Holy Spirit, into his conscience.

Just as I am certain that the devil speaks to us, I am also convinced that God speaks. But God does a better job at getting through. The Bible promises, "The One who is in you is greater than the one who is in the world" (1 John 4:4). Susan must have faith that God was at work in Glen's life before she came around, and God will continue being at work in the future. Her role, therefore, is to echo the voice of God, Who is already speaking to Glen's conscience. That is how she can be used by God, rather than used to enable.

On the topic of leaving as it relates to parenting, your first reaction may be to say to your kids, "You can leave." But there are a variety of levels of leaving, from mild to severe, which parents may experience. Some of these are so severe that readers may be shocked to see them on this list. But I include them because they are realistic in the sense that they really do happen. In addition, if we remain absolutely committed to the criterion that our primary role is to disciple our children, and we decide which of the options for relational change we should employ based on what is in the best interest of the other person, some of these instances of leaving ought to remain "on the table."

You may have to walk away just because you are so angry that this is the only way to maintain self-control. But if you do, your decision to walk away is nonetheless impulsive and not necessarily a conscious decision of what's best for your child's discipleship. It is possible to walk away even if you are not angry and even if you don't need to "let off steam." Your reason for leaving may be to "let off steam." You realize that if you continue the conversation, you or your kids are just going to let your feelings escalate, so leaving is your best immediate option.

Maybe your reason for leaving is to allow them to fail, and you think this will be valuable for their discipleship. Or perhaps you may choose to leave simply as an act of grace. But I believe that on some occasions, the best instruction is an exhibition of grace. That is why the decision-making criterion among the nine options for relational change is not what you find easiest, what you think will work, what you are best at, or what you prefer, but what is best for the other person. You may find occasions where what is best for the other person is grace. But that grace must be "grace with strength."

In Jude 23 we read, "Show mercy, mixed with fear." Every time we show mercy to someone, we do so at a price. To show mercy means that we don't inflict the consequences that someone else deserves.

Showing mercy is a God-like act. God is merciful. As people who unrelentingly reflect God's image, we should also show mercy.

What's more, showing mercy is fair. We have all received plenty of mercy from God and from others for the sins that we have committed. Certainly, if others show mercy to us, we can return the favor. But every time we show mercy, there is a risk. When the other person is spared the consequences, they may learn an unintended lesson: "I can get away with it. No big deal."

This doesn't mean that we should avoid mercy. God isn't stingy in showing mercy, and He is fully aware of the risk. When Jesus died on the cross and declared that the punishment we deserved was paid in full, He ran the risk of us getting the idea that we could keep on sinning. But He did it anyway. That's why Jude says, "Show mercy, mixed with fear." When we show mercy, we should also be mindful that the person who is spared his punishment may also be spared true repentance.

So how do we find the right balance between mercy and fear? Whenever we extend mercy or grace, it should be done as an intentional act. We don't show mercy simply because we are too lazy to inflict consequences. We don't extend grace simply because we are afraid of the other person's reaction if we confront them. Instead, true grace is an act of tremendous strength. It means that you are fully willing and prepared to confront the other person, but you consciously decide that a display of grace is better for their discipleship. At that moment, you believe grace is consistent with the character of God, even though discipline is also consistent with God's character.

There are some extreme cases where temporary separation from children can be a selfless act in their best interest. It is conceivable that, for some children, the place most suited to their discipleship is juvenile hall if they have committed some crime when they should have known better—especially if that criminal activity has been repeated.

Similarly, I know a couple whose daughter, Brianna, became so defiant that, after repeated efforts to address her behavior, they felt their best option was to send her to "boot camp." She lived in a snowy part of Utah for three months. When she returned, she had a renewed respect for authority, and especially for her parents.

Some older teenagers also reach a point of defiance and recklessness that legal emancipation becomes an unfortunate, yet important, tool in their discipleship. In each of these heart-wrenching decisions, parents decide that they must let their children experience hardship as part of their growth.

Obviously, there are some parents who have just "had it" with their kids and they send them to boarding school or boot camp to get rid of them. But some wise parents see that their children must be allowed to experience the consequences of their actions in order to help them ultimately to succeed.

Fortunately, many parents will not likely face any of those drastic decisions or options. But I start with them because I want to establish that if you as a parent can envision temporarily separating your children as an act of love, then surely you can envision something less drastic like walking out of the room as also loving. There may be times where the best instruction you can give your kids is to leave, hang up, or end the conversation.

WHAT LEAVING LOOKS LIKE IN FRIENDSHIP

Jim became a Christian at the age of 26, after spending 10 years devoted to drinking and partying. Like many new Christians, he wondered whether his new life in Christ demanded that he put an end to his former friendships. This is not an easy question to answer because the biblical answer is, "It depends." In the words of the Apostle Paul:

> I wrote to you in my letter not to associate with sexually immoral people—not at all meaning the people of this world who are immoral, or the greedy and swindlers, or idolaters. In that case you would have to leave this world. But now I am writing to you that you must not associate with anyone who claims to be a brother or sister but is sexually immoral or greedy, an idolater or slanderer, a drunkard or swindler. Do not even eat with such people (1 Cor. 5:9-11).

In other words, it is impossible to stop associating with immoral people altogether because we would have to leave this planet. Nor should we stop associating with non-Christians who are immoral because we can be a light to them. Yet, some Christians do not have the required willpower to be a witness to their former immoral friends. So in the case of non-Christians, whether a new believer can continue these friendships depends on his ability to keep "bad company [from] corrupt[ing] good character" (1 Cor. 15:33).

Paul's message in 1 Corinthians 5 is clear in that Christians should not associate with other Christians who refuse to repent of immoral behavior. That's because the lack of fellowship is designed to bring the other person to repentance or to the realization that they are not truly a Christian.

Based on these passages, there are a few instances where it would be best for a friend to "leave" his or her other friends. Here are a few examples:

- It is better to leave if you cannot refrain from sinning when you are around these friends.
- It is better to leave if your fellowship gives the other person the impression that immoral behavior is acceptable for Christians.
- It is better to leave if your fellowship gives the other person the false impression that they are a Christian.
- It is better to leave if associating with the other person is unbearably painful for you because the other person continues to hurt you.

The last point deserves an example for explanation. Karen had a friend named Bren, who held a grudge which she continually brought up when they were together. Years ago, Karen was watching Bren's children at her friend's house in the country. Bren told her not to let the cat out because the cars drove too quickly in front of the farmhouse, and the cat could get struck. That very evening, Karen accidentally did let the cat out, and, tragically, it was killed by a car. Bren brought up this story often, sometimes explicitly, and other times with implied remarks about "irresponsibility" or "carelessness."

But even when Bren didn't address the incident with words, she continually seemed angry, unforgiving, and hostile. It got to the point where Karen felt pain every time she got together with Bren. She finally realized that, even though friendship requires openness, her vulnerability was mainly exposing her to pain, not growth or love. She told Bren that she would have to take a six-month break from speaking with her because she needed to protect herself from the pain.

There are times where the most loving thing to do is to leave. You begin with a clear plan, timeline, and purpose. You explain to the person you love what you plan to do, why, for how long. Whether it's hanging up the phone, walking out of the room, or something more significant, you communicate the relationship is in need of change. And you can do this in love.

CHAPTER 7

MAKE A BOUNDARY

BACK TO MARIE AGAIN: BOUNDARIES also facilitate relational change. Marie could establish a boundary with her mother. She could express a rule or expectation and then state what consequences will occur if her mother violates it. For instance, she could say:

- "I expect help with cleaning the bathroom. If I have to clean it myself, I will deduct $50 a month from my rent as compensation for my time."
- "I need to live with a cleaner bathroom. I will have to move out next month if I cannot get your help this month."
- "We have two bathrooms in this house, and I am the only person cleaning them. If I cannot get your help, I expect to have the use of one bathroom, while you use the other."

We all know boundaries can be incredibly helpful, indeed wonderful, and are usually there for a reason. I visited a Dutch family in Ghana several years ago, and they told me to make myself at home. As I walked down a hallway, I was impressed that all the doors on the home were cutely painted with labels, such as "Kitchen," "Bathroom," etc. One of the doors was labeled, "Joke." I'm always up for a good joke, so I tugged on the door, expecting to see a wall immediately behind the door. Instead, I saw a bedroom, and then I glanced at my host's faces and realized I had just committed a faux pas. Then it occurred to me—the couple was named Anders and Joke (a Dutch name pronounced *Yo-Ka*). I had just helped myself into her room. That was a boundary I wasn't supposed to cross.

The Bible says, "I will walk about in freedom, for I have sought out your precepts" (Ps. 119:45). Ironically, the psalmist sees that there is greater freedom to walk because he stays within the bounds of the law. The boundaries create freedom. This is also true in relationships. You can get untrapped by establishing clearer boundaries.

DEFINITION OF "MAKE A BOUNDARY"

"Establishing what consequences will occur if the other person violates your rule."

PUNISHING: THE NEGATIVE COUSIN OF BOUNDARIES

Rather than establish purposeful boundaries, we have a tendency to punish. For example:

- I'm never going to lend him money again.
- I'm not going to return his phone call or emails.
- I won't let her borrow anything again.
- I'll never help him with a project at work or school.
- I'll gossip, so others know how bad they are.
- I'll tattle, so they get in trouble at school, work, or home.
- I'll shame them by ridicule, so others know how bad of a person he or she is.

We have a variety of ways to punish the people around us. We can make sarcastic remarks like, "Wow. It has taken two weeks for the bathroom to look like this. Normally, it's this disgusting within one week." Or we ask punishing questions like, "Don't you feel bad that I have to do all this work myself?" Or we punish by creating a standoff: "I refuse to clean the bathroom, and we'll see how long it goes before you finally give in." Or we ask shaming questions like, "Do you know anyone else who lives like this?" We might try punishing actions like creating a mess for someone else to clean up, so they can see how it feels.

One of the problems with punishing is that it usually does not effect change. People often have a difficult time reading between the lines of our sarcastic or punishing comments. They are absorbed in their own emotions and worldview, so they need us to clearly spell out our own. The type of punishing I am describing here is not instructive. It does not help people grow.

Another problem is that it doesn't make you feel better. By expressing anger or frustration, you don't really have a "catharsis" where you let off the steam. Instead, by exercising your anger in this way, you actually cultivate contempt. Since there is no resolution or understanding, you continue to let the anger fester.

WHAT BOUNDARIES LOOK LIKE IN THE BIBLE

God makes boundaries with us. In the Bible, He tells us where He draws the line and what consequences will occur. There are numerous examples of this throughout scripture. A prominent one regards those who would enter the Promised Land.

Moses wandered through the desert for 40 years with over a million Israelites. This assembly awaited the land flowing with milk and honey, but they failed to trust God. Later, Moses sent spies into the land of Canaan (one of the regions he was supposed to conquer), but the report caused the people to lose heart. Only two men (Joshua and Caleb) had faith that God was going to deliver on His promise. So we read of the consequences: "Not one of you will enter the land I swore with uplifted hand to make your home, except Caleb son of Jephunneh and Joshua son of Nun" (Num. 14:30).

The Bible begins with God making a boundary with humankind. God told Adam he could eat of any tree in the Garden of Eden except the tree of the knowledge of good and evil. Regarding that tree, God said, "For when you eat from it, you will certainly die" (Gen. 2:17). God clearly established these two things: where the line is (do not eat the fruit), and what will happen if someone crosses that line (you will surely die). Then God lived up to His word—physical death entered humanity, and spiritual death did as well.

Many of us find it difficult to clearly state where we draw the line in our boundaries with other people. Even fewer of us are clear what consequences will result. And even fewer still have the strength to live up to that promise.

King David knew what it was like to cross a boundary and incur the consequences. God made it clear to David that going to war should only be God's prerogative. God did not want David to be presumptuous, assuming that he could go to war whenever he desired. That's because God didn't want David thinking his success was a result of his own strength. And it's also because God wanted the victories of Israel to glorify His name, create a people for Himself, and exercise judgment on people who were wicked.

But we read in 1 Chronicles 21 that David "numbered his troops." This does not sound particularly terrible. Since when was counting a sin? But when a king counts his troops, he's up to something. And God knew it was in David's heart to go to war, even though God had not commanded it. So God explained to David that he had crossed the boundary, and there would be consequences.

In this case, God gave David a choice: he could have three days of plague or three months of running from his enemies. David reasoned that it was better to fall into the hands of God than the hands of his enemies, since God might be merciful. So David chose plague. And God implemented these consequences, which were severe.

God had each of the options in this book at His disposal in dealing with David's sin. He could have done nothing. He could have withdrawn His blessing from David, meaning He could have left David. He could have instructed the king. But in this case, I take it that God used the same criterion I offer here, "What was in David's best interest? What was in Israel's best interest?" Leaving, listening, teaching, and offering grace can all be in the best interest of others. But to fail to implement the consequences of crossing the line can be very unloving.

Some people mistakenly think that the reason they must draw boundaries is so that, "Other people won't walk all over them." It is true that God does not want you to be walked on like a doormat, and it is unhealthy for you to let people take advantage of you. But that is not the primary reason we draw boundaries. We do it because it is unhealthy for others not to have boundaries. It is unhealthy for your sister when you let your sister walk all over you. We draw boundaries because it is in the best interest of the other person.

Boundaries often come in the form of discipline. Discipline is usually a function of parenting. As our Father, God disciplines the children He loves. The author of Hebrews argues that discipline is a proof of God's love: "If you are not disciplined—and everyone undergoes discipline—then you are not legitimate, not true sons and daughters at all" (Heb. 12:8). Not only does discipline prove God's love, it also proves that we are God's children. God wouldn't bother disciplining us if He didn't love us or if we weren't His children because He would write us off as a lost cause.

Hebrews explains the value of discipline: "No discipline seems pleasant at the time, but painful. Later on, however, it produces a harvest of righteousness and peace for those who have been trained by it" (Heb. 12:11).

Since discipline is an expression of love, the Bible repeatedly encourages parents to discipline children. We read, "Discipline your children, for in that there is hope; do not be a willing party to their death" (Prov. 19:18).

You may be wondering, why is this section entitled "Make a Boundary" rather than "Discipline"? My simple answer to that is we generally reserve the word "discipline" for the role of parents in the lives of their children. But establishing boundaries is a vital element for all relationships. It is something people must learn to do regardless of the power differential between them. Nevertheless, there is a strong similarity between discipline and boundaries. Both concepts convey the desire to communicate truth through consequences. I see discipline and boundaries as similar concepts, but the word "boundary" is more applicable to all of our relationships. Unlike the chapter on "teaching" where we state the truth and the consequences, in this chapter we intend to create the consequences if our rule is broken.

WHAT BOUNDARIES LOOK LIKE IN MARRIAGE

Boundaries are vital to a healthy marriage. In order to experience relational change, you will need to have the skill of making boundaries. People hesitate to draw boundaries in marriage because they do not associate boundaries with love. But the opposite is true: love is always circumscribed by boundaries.

To see the relationship between love and boundaries, read completely through Psalm 119. The Psalm repeats the theme of love and law/command/boundary. Consider verse 45: "I will walk about in freedom, for I have sought out your precepts." How is the psalmist able to walk in freedom? Because the boundaries are clearly drawn!

In a hilarious Seinfeld episode, Kramer "adopted a highway" and took this relationship too seriously. He began by picking up trash but then decided his mile was going to be the Cadillac of driving experience—one super wide lane. This caused confusion and chaos, culminating in explosion and disaster.

The lines on a road enable the drivers to have freedom. Because of the boundaries, they are at peace. The stricter the lines, the more at liberty the driver is to speed! In California, we have some High Occupancy lanes with four yellow stripes and a $401 minimum penalty for crossing over. The drivers in that lane have the greatest liberty to drive the fastest with the least fear of crashing.

Your marriage will have greater freedom with better boundaries because boundaries build trust and remedy or address areas of distrust.

Boundaries can be drawn by words or by deeds. Following is a list of ways a partner can make a boundary by actions:

- Leaving for the party alone when the perpetually late partner doesn't come home by the agreed upon departure time,
- Going ahead and eating dinner when a spouse is late for the "thousandth" time,
- Ending an abusive conversation,
- Refusing to bail someone out of a jam because of perpetual irresponsibility like overspending or not completing work on time,
- Removing oneself from an argument or heated situation,
- Taking some time away from one another to sort things out,
- Moving out to get treatment for an addiction,
- Separating from physical abuse or substance abuse,
- Moving into a shelter to protect children,
- Using a third party to help you resolve conflict, or
- Giving yourself an allotted time to talk about certain things.[50]

Boundaries can also be drawn by the things you say. Following is a list of things you can say to make a boundary:

- "I love you, but I don't trust you. I can't be that close again until we work this out."
- "When you can be kind, we can be close again."
- "When you show you are serious about getting some help, I will feel safe enough to open up to you again."

---

50 Cloud and Townsend, *Boundaries in Marriage*, 30-33.

- "I can't share deep feelings if you are going to punish me for them."[51]
- "Honey, you have a mean side, and it makes me distance myself from you. I love you, but I won't subject myself to this treatment. I want you to work on this issue with me so it doesn't happen again."[52]
- "Honey, when I tell you my negative feelings, it hurts me that you become critical of me and focus the issue on yourself. This makes me withdraw from you. I want and need to be close to you, and I will work toward this. But if you continue to negate me instead of hear me, I may need to distance somewhat and take those deeper feelings to friends who will try to understand me."[53]
- "I love you, and I want you to be with me and the kids for dinner, but if you can't get here in time, I will have your dinner put away in the fridge. You can reheat it yourself whenever you get in."[54]

Each of these statements draws a respectful boundary, and thereby overcomes the tendency for us to either be too passive or too demanding. These statements strike a balance of truth and love and empower both people to have a healthy relationship.

WHAT BOUNDARIES LOOK LIKE IN PARENTING

The primary way parents discipline children is by drawing boundaries. Often, the attempt to make a boundary fails because an

---

51 Cloud and Townsend, *Boundaries in Marriage*, 32.
52 Cloud and Townsend, *Boundaries in Marriage*, 53.
53 Cloud and Townsend, *Boundaries in Marriage*, 58.
54 Cloud and Townsend, *Boundaries in Marriage*, 61.

unwinnable power struggle ensues. Parents make unenforceable demands or vague commands. Parents relent because they realize they created an unreasonable standoff. And sometimes parents are hesitant to exercise power over their children because they lack an understanding or justification for why they should make demands at all. As Tedd Tripp explains, "Parents in our culture often improvise because they do not understand the biblical mandate to shepherd children."[55]

Unfortunately, many parents approach parenting with an attitude that they will "figure it out as they go along." Without a solid understanding of the role you play in your kids' lives, you will miss God-given opportunities for relational change.

Boundaries enclose; they circumscribe something important. The boundary paint on a highway determines the center of a road. The boundary circles on a target create the bull's eye. Your boundaries as a parent reveal your bull's eye. Without prior thought or development of a philosophy (or theology) of parenting, your bull's eye will seem arbitrary to you and your kids. At times, the boundaries you set will create an implicit bull's eye of "making me happy." Other times you will draw the boundaries around the center of "not embarrassing me." With the bull's eye undefined, your boundaries are likely to fail. Or you are likely to change them because you haven't fully committed to what goal you were hoping your boundaries would accomplish.

Following are four foundational rules for setting boundaries with children. These rules will help you set up enforceable, reasonable boundaries. Even better, these rules give focus to boundaries.

RULE 1: COMMUNICATE A THEOLOGY

Many of the things parents say to their kids set the bar shamefully low. Parents give rules to kids that often appeal to power, the preference of the parents, or at best, the extreme consequences of their actions. But if parents have an instructive role in the lives of their children, power and preference are irrelevant. What matters is sin and righteousness. The following statements reveal how low we often set the bar:

- "Don't have sex before you are married, or you could get [yourself/your girlfriend] pregnant."
- "Go to bed, or you'll be sleepy in the morning."
- "Get your homework done, or your grades will suffer."

In each of these cases, the rule is too shortsighted. So much more could be said! Aiming the bar for holiness and right standing with God, similar, yet better, instruction would sound like:

- "Sex before marriage will rob you of the wonderful reward God has in store for the righteous."
- "Going to bed when you are asked is a sign of an obedient heart, which is vital for a right relationship with God and your parents."
- "Doing your homework is an act of obedience and develops godly character."

When our son, Sonny, was younger, he would take his Nintendo DS into the bathroom. It was easy for him to get lost in the game and lose track of time when he did this. Sometimes while he was in the middle of his homework, he would grab his DS, head to the bathroom, and not return for a half an hour.

My wife and I considered how to address this. We came up with a few options:

- We could have a "no DS in the bathroom rule."
- We could tell him, "Don't spend any more time in the bathroom than you need to."
- We could say, "You're not allowed to go to the bathroom until you are done with your homework."

The problem with these options is that they miss the heart of the issue. He was using the excuse of being in the bathroom as an excuse to play when he should have been doing homework, chores, or socializing with the family. If we made a "no DS in the bathroom rule," we would only address one specific behavior. That rule would in no way touch on the other issues, such as obediently doing homework or socializing with the family.

If we said, "Don't spend more time in the bathroom than you need to," we would set ourselves up for failure because this is an indefinable amount of time and an unenforceable command. We would not know how much time was necessary!

And if we said, "You're not allowed to go to the bathroom until you are done with your homework," we would likely reverse ourselves when he complained of urgency. Nearly every parent will lose a standoff about whether a child can go to the bathroom.

What we really wanted to say to our son had very little to do with whether he brought a DS into the bathroom. The most important messages we wanted to communicate were:

- "It is disobedient and dishonest to use the bathroom as an excuse to play, rather than do your homework."
- "Acting deceitfully hardens your heart and keeps you from having a right relationship with God and with us."

In making boundaries, especially with children, we must start by thinking theologically. In what way does God want you to instruct your child? What truth empowers you to discipline at this point in time? What truth do you need to convey through your discipline? Implicitly, every parenting expert, parent and child knows the following:

Parenting without theology is merely an exercise of power.

Kids know this; parents know it; and every author of a parenting book knows it. But people respond to that truth in a variety of ways. Children respond by saying, "I'm up for the challenge!" Often parents respond in fear, thinking, "I don't want to be more powerful than my kids; I just want to love them and care for them." So they shy away from parenting with authority because a power struggle doesn't sound nurturing. And some parenting experts suggest that it is oppressive for people to exercise power over others, no matter how much larger or older they are. For them, power-plays are violent.

But there is another option. Parenting *without* theology is merely an exercise of power. If you do not have a theology of who you are in the life of your child, what right do you have to tell them what to do? Because you are bigger? That's oppressive. Because you are older? That doesn't necessarily make you wiser. Because you are wiser? By whose definition? Parents are often crippled because they don't know what gives them the right to discipline and teach their kids.

What gives you the right is answered in good theology. You have the right to instruct—not because you are older, bigger, or the bread winner, but because the family is God's design for instruction. As the parent, God has designed your role for you to shepherd your kids and teach them. You cannot abdicate this responsibility even if you feel inadequate or afraid. God did not assign this role to anyone else.

Once you have a theology of who you are (God's instrument of instruction and nurture), you also need a theology of sin and discipline. How many spankings is a lie worth? How many minutes in time out is hitting worth? The purpose of discipline is not payment, but teaching. It illustrates a truth—that there is a breach in relationship (time out) and that sin causes pain (spanking). A lie cannot be paid for by one spanking or by 10. And when a child hits his brother, neither 10 minutes nor 10 hours in time out is enough to pay for the sin. So we must get over the idea that the only form of discipline is the natural consequences.

Discipline should be instructive, rather than retributive. The purpose of spanking a child once for a lie is to illustrate to the child that they sinned. Subsequent spankings are not needed to illustrate this truth. The spanking may cause a little pain, which is what sin causes. The spanking should be accompanied with teaching: "You lied to me. Lying is a sin. I am spanking you because you sinned. [spank]. I forgive you for lying, and I love you."

Similarly, when a child hits his brother, no specific amount of time in his room will pay for that sin. But 10 or 15 minutes in his room may illustrate a truth about sin. Sin causes separation. Sin causes relational estrangement. This is a theological truth that empowers you to discipline, but it should be made explicit as theological instruction to the child: "You hit your brother. Hitting is a sin. You need to repent of your sin. You will spend 10 minutes in your room for time-out. [Ten minutes later]. I forgive you for hitting, and I love you."

As the resident theologian in your home, you don't have to ask the question, "Why did you hit your sister?" You know the answer. Johnnie hit his sister because his heart is wicked, like your heart and my heart. He hit his sister because he sins. Rather than ask your kids questions that they don't know the answer to, it is your job to instruct them with the deeper answers you do know. Teach them from a young age to think theologically about their behavior and what it says about their heart.

If you do not think theologically about your role of instruction regarding sin and repentance, your discipline will be:

- Setting the bar low,
- Unprepared to win standoffs with your kids,
- Crippled by fear of a power struggle, and
- Behaviorally-focused, rather than heart-focused.

RULE 2: WIN

One of the principles by which my wife and I have determined to live is never to ask anything of our kids that we can*not* enforce. There are a few reasons we are so determined to win. The first is theological—if we make demands that our kids fail to keep, we implicitly teach them that our authority is impotent. They might then get the impression that it is acceptable to disobey authority, which could lead to the biblical condition known as "hardness of heart."

God allowed Pharaoh to disobey His repeated demand to let the Israelites go. But that is because God hardened Pharaoh's heart, treating him as a "lost cause." God has the wisdom to know that Pharaoh was a lost cause, but it is our responsibility as parents to prevent our children from hardness of heart.

Another more pragmatic reason we don't have expectations that we are unable to enforce is to prevent frustrating power struggles. You can't, for instance, *make* a child eat his dinner. You can ask, but you can't enforce this demand. Some parents swear that they will make their child sit at the dinner table until the food is gone. I've found that kids typically win these stand-offs. Parents are generally gracious people, overwhelmed with pity and eventually warmed by their children's charm that is hidden behind sassy attitudes. Besides, parents and children both know that this threat is unreasonable, should the stand-off last more than several hours. Similarly, you can't make a kid:

- Fall asleep,
- Answer a question,
- Tell the truth,
- Eat,
- Do their homework, or
- Apologize.

This doesn't mean we are powerless; it just means we have to make slight adjustments in what we ask, to ensure that we will maintain legitimate authority. Here is what we can enforce:

- "You need to stay in your bed. If not, I will pick you up and put you in time-out, and then I'll put you in your bed."
- "If you do not answer the question, you will go to time out for being disrespectful."
- "If you do not tell me the truth, you will get a spanking." (But you cannot then demand the child tell you the truth because you can't enforce that.)
- "If you do not eat your dinner, you will not get dessert."

- "You need to stay at this desk until your homework is done. If it is not done in an hour, you will not go out with your friends on the weekend."
- "You need to apologize, or you will go to time out."

This principle is the primary theme of *Parenting with Love and Logic*. Foster Cline and Jim Fay explain that the natural consequences of actions often serve as sufficient instruction. The key to optimizing the teachability of consequences is to frame the choices correctly. They write:

> If a toddler is acting inappropriately the parent can . . . give him a choice: 'Would you like to go to your room walking, or would you like me to carry you?' Notice that the parent is not telling the child how to act, such as 'stop that right now!' Such a statement is not enforceable; all it means is that the parent will have to act again if the behavior continues.[56]

RULE 3: SHEPHERD THE HEART

This point was largely covered in chapter one, where we looked at the central role of instruction in parenting. I have contended for each of the nine options of relational change that they should support the primary goal of communicating truth. Boundaries in parenting (discipline) should be instructive. They should communicate truth.

Tedd Tripp explains the basic purpose of boundaries:

> If correction orbits around the parent who has been offended, then the focus will be venting anger or, perhaps, taking vengeance. The function is punitive. If, however, correction orbits around God as the one offended, then the focus is restoration. The function is remedial. It is designed

---

56 Cline and Fay, *Parenting with Love and Logic*, 57.

to move a child who has disobeyed God back to the path of obedience. It is corrective.[57]

The goal of discipline is to teach children the truth and consequence of their behavior. The truth is deeper than, "I get irritated when you are rude to your sister." The truth is that each of us, including our children, sins against God. Our sin stems from a deceitful and rebellious heart. And our hearts need to change in order for our behavior to change. The change of heart, coupled with the change of behavior, is what the Bible calls repentance.

Tedd Tripp examines the various goals that parents have for their kids: developing special skills, adjusting psychologically, being well-behaved children, obtaining a good education, and having control. While all of these are desirable, he reminds us of the true primary goal: "Teaching your children to live for the glory of God must be your overarching objective . . . if you accept this goal as the only one worthy of your attention and effort, what methods must you employ to help them embrace this goal for living?"[58]

Jesus said, "The mouth speaks what the heart is full of" (Matt. 12:34). Our children's behavior is an indication of what is going on in their heart. Our primary concern should be what is going on in their heart, and therefore, when we observe misbehavior, we should count it as an opportunity, rather than merely as a frustration. My friend Sean put it this way, "I was thankful when my daughter sinned last week because I was able to have a window into her soul. And I took the opportunity to address what was in her heart. She repented, and I'm so glad I noticed the sin!"

---

57 Tripp, *Shepherding a Child's Heart*, 36.
58 Tripp, *Shepherding a Child's Heart*, 56.

RULE 4: BE CONSISTENT

Nearly all parenting experts iterate this point. Even if people are unconscious or neglectful of the central role of theology in parenting or the importance of shepherding the heart, we all know that behavior modification is useless unless it is consistent. When I was in my 20s, I took a cross country drive with my Australian friend Troy. I did most of the driving and sped nearly every mile of the trip. After about 500 miles I said, "Do you speed when you drive?" Kindly, he said, "No, but I won't judge you if you do."

I was grateful about the lack of judgment but incredulous that he didn't speed. "Ever?" I said.

"No, in Australia, you get a ticket every time you speed. There are cameras everywhere."

Needless to say, we can all see that even a cheap ticket consistently given is more effective at behavior modification than an expensive ticket incurred every few years. But as parents who shepherd the heart, behavior modification is only a small portion of our task. Our job is not to modify behavior so that our kids are tolerable or so they don't make us crazy. Our job is to consistently instruct the heart. Tripp writes:

> Obedience to parents is not a parent-child issue. If it were, the parent could be selective about when he wished to be obeyed. Obedience is not simply between the parent and the child. It is an issue between the child and God in which the parent is God's agent in drawing the child back within the circle of blessing.[59]

As God's vessel of instruction, we do not have the luxury of deciding when to be consistent about discipline based on our energy level or our level of irritation. We are at all times charged with the responsibility of shepherding the heart.

---

59 Tripp, *Shepherding a Child's Heart*, 136.

WHAT BOUNDARIES LOOK
LIKE IN FRIENDSHIP

There is a direct relationship between intimacy and the need for boundaries. The closer you are to your friends, the more need for boundaries you will discover. We all know that the people most capable of hurting us are the people who know us the best. So boundaries in friendship are vital to continued health in the relationship. The "boundary experts," Henry Cloud and John Townsend, offer several examples of what boundaries in friendship sound like, such as:

- "I'm sorry that you have not done that before now, and I understand that you are in a bind. Maybe next time you will plan better. That's not my job."[60]

- "You hired me for 20 hours a week, and you have just given me about 40 hours of work. Which 20 would you like done?"[61]

- Here is a list of a few more boundaries you may have to draw with the people you love:

- "I will cover half the cost of this repair, but I expect you to pay the other half."

- "I will not speak with you for a week because I feel hurt and need some time."

- "I will not be as vulnerable, open, or communicative with you until I feel safer with you."

- "I will not be able to leave my kids at your home until you lock your pool gate."

---

60 Cloud and Townsend, *Boundaries*, 196.
61 Cloud and Townsend, *Boundaries*, 197.

- "I will not be responding to emails that seem accusatory. I will have these conversations face to face."
- "I am going to tell your wife/husband about this situation."
- "I will not lend this item to you."
- "We will bring our children to your home when a pornography filter is installed on the computer."
- "I will not have time to help you this week."

In each of these instances, we draw a clear boundary, motivated by our love for the other person. Each statement asks, "What is best for the other person?" and answers that question with "Saying no."

THE SPIRITUAL REALITY OF CONFLICT

Whenever we draw a boundary with someone, conflict is inevitable. The very fact that you feel the need to draw a boundary indicates that it will be unwelcome by the other person. It is helpful to remember throughout the ensuing struggle that our battle is not with the other person. The other person is not your enemy. On the contrary, your boundary is an act of love.

For a brief period when my younger son, Micah, was ten years old, he went through a rather violent phase. My wife called me to come home from work because he was hitting her and resisting any form of punishment. He was making it impossible to spank him or even restrain him. I knew I needed to oppose him, but I also knew this needed to be done carefully because I am aware that my "struggle is not against flesh and blood, but against the authorities, against the powers of this dark world and against the spiritual forces of evil in the heavenly realms" (Eph. 6:12).

So when I came home from work, I knew I was in for a battle, but I considered that the battle was not with my son. I heard that he was likely to kick and punch when I came in to his room, but I knew that my struggle was not with him. I envisioned instead that my son and I were struggling together, against the spiritual attack that our home was under. Satan desired "to steal, kill, and destroy" (Jn. 10:10), to "sift him like wheat" as Jesus said to Peter (Lk. 22:31). But I knew the Lord, and my son, wanted victory over the devil (even if my son wasn't aware of the struggle in that way).

I did have to carefully restrain him on the ground. It was one of the most difficult things I have ever done—not that he was a particularly strong ten-year-old, but it was a heart-breaking struggle to be having in the first place. What made it bearable is that I remembered the story of Jacob, who wrestled with an angel (Gen. 32).

There are some things that are not parallel in the story: I am not an angel. And in the Bible, Jacob was victorious, but my son was restrained. Nevertheless, there are some important similarities. My son did struggle with me, and after the struggle, he experienced a kind of victory. After Jacob wrestled with the angel, the Lord changed his name to "Israel," which means, "He will be victorious." I felt like my son was Israel at the end of that struggle. Though I restrained him, he was victorious. He was the victor because he and I struggled together against Satan, and together we won the spiritual battle. My son's will was broken, but the devil did not "steal, kill, or destroy" his spirit. He changed that day and was never violent like that again. I credit this, in part, to exercising solidarity with him and reminding him that we never "struggle against flesh and blood" (Eph. 6:12).

CHAPTER 8

COMPROMISE

MARIE COULD COMPROMISE. SHE COULD work something out with her mother and sister where they share the work. Marie could clean the bathroom on Tuesdays; her mother could clean it on Thursdays; and her sister could clean it on Saturdays.

Compromise need not be exactly fair, though. Evidently, for Marie to clean the bathroom "costs" her less than for her mother or sister. So she could clean the bathroom three weeks of the month and ask her mother and sister to clean it on the last week of the month. This may represent a more accurate "cost of difficulty" or sacrifice.

If you suggested this to Marie, she would probably retort, "My sister and mother will never live up to their agreement. This won't last a month." That is possibly true, but it is not the criterion suggested in this book for how to decide which positive option to pursue. Marie should only compromise if she thinks going about that decision is in her mother's and sister's best interest. Coming to this agreement of compromise could be incredibly valuable, even if her mother and sister fail to live up to their end of the deal. It could illustrate a variety of things to Marie or to her family:

- It could show how unfair the situation is that Marie has to do all the work.

- When Marie cleans the bathroom, it could serve to teach what a clean bathroom looks like.

- It could show Marie that her mother is truly incapable of doing this work for some reason—depression or mental illness, for example.

- It could give Marie the clarity that she needs to decide whether to move out, do nothing, or sacrifice and clean it herself from now on.

- It could give Marie's mother and sister the final motivation to start helping out.

Compromise can accomplish a variety of things, but we need to be clear what we are trying to gain when we pursue this option. Generally, if you ask people what they are trying to accomplish by compromising, they will say, "We want to make both parties happy." This rarely works because, in most compromises, both people give something up. Happiness cannot be the end in itself. Compromise may, instead, accomplish other valuable purposes which indirectly increase happiness. It may increase understanding; it may demonstrate solidarity; or it may serve to teach something.

DEFINITION OF "COMPROMISE"

"The intentional decision for two or more people to partially give up a desire."

One reason we must learn to compromise in order to get untrapped is that it seems we are all playing by different rules or maybe even a different game altogether! My wife, Kristina, owns a small party rental company, so she receives quite a few checks as payment. Very few of these checks have ever bounced; she has a great customer base. But one time, a check bounced, so Kristina called the customer to ask about arranging payment.

The client asked her, "What day did you cash the check?"

"Tuesday," my wife said.

"Well, that's your problem," the customer informed her. "You need to do it on Friday. Early. Try it again this Friday morning, and it will go through."

She said it in a way that was self-evident, as if everyone knew that you were supposed to deposit checks on Fridays. Apparently, Friday is her payday, and Friday mornings are a feeding frenzy with "first come, first served" in her bank account. We realized in this encounter that some things seem normal to us and bizarre to others, and vice versa. With such a thought in mind, we must get better at compromise.

Compromise and sacrifice seem similar. When you sacrifice, you give up something that is important to you. And when you compromise, you must also give up something important to you. The difference, however, is that sacrifice is unilateral. It does not require anything of the other person. You can sacrifice, whether the other person knows, cares, or even wants you to do so.

Compromise requires both people to work together. Both must sacrifice. The fact that both people must work together doesn't make compromise "better" than sacrifice. Each has its advantages and disadvantages.

When you compromise, both people lose something; but when you sacrifice, only one person "loses." Sacrifice, however, should be done joyfully, so it is not really a loss. Sacrifice is safer than compromise in the sense that you invest in something that is within your control (you will either sacrifice or not). Compromise is risky because the other person may not work with you or may not keep their end of the deal. But sacrifice is also risky because you give up something you value completely, while compromise has the safety of letting you keep a part of what you value.

BARGAINING: THE NEGATIVE COUSIN OF COMPROMISING

Compromise can seem similar to bargaining. But bargaining is manipulative rather than cooperative. When you bargain, you keep trying to win. Instead, the criterion suggested in this book is that we ask what is in the other person's best interest.

Sometimes compromise is terrible for the other person. No one wants a friend who agrees to lie "some of the time" or a husband who will be sexually faithful "except on Mardi Gras."

Often, my wife and I try to decide where to go to eat. I'll usually suggest Mexican food, and she'll suggest Japanese food. It doesn't make sense for us to do Italian instead. This would be a lose-lose situation, where neither of us gets something we want. And since she can't find anything on a Mexican food menu that she wants to eat, it doesn't make sense for us to alternate Mexican one week with Japanese the next. I need to find other opportunities to get my Mexican food "fix" besides going out to dinner with her.

Sometimes, however, compromise really is best for the other person.

WHAT COMPROMISE LOOKS LIKE IN THE BIBLE

Apparently, even God is not beyond compromise. In the book of Isaiah, we read that the prophet told King Hezekiah, "This is what the LORD says: Put your house in order, because you are going to die;

you will not recover" (Is. 38:1). Hezekiah had presided over a nation that was increasingly given to idolatry. God prepared the neighboring nation of Assyria as an instrument of punishment to come and temporarily destroy Israel. Hezekiah understood from the prophets that this was going to happen.

But when he became ill, he humbled himself, and he begged God not to let him die. He prayed, "Remember, LORD, how I have walked before you faithfully and with wholehearted devotion and have done what is good in your eyes" (Is. 38:3).

Isaiah tells us, "Then the word of the LORD came to Isaiah: 'Go and tell Hezekiah, 'This is what the LORD, the God of your father David, says: I have heard your prayer and seen your tears; I will add 15 years to your life" (Is. 38:4-5).

We don't really know why God did this for Hezekiah. The nation was still destroyed at the hands of Assyria, and Hezekiah's family suffered the same fate. Surely God knew the future: that Hezekiah would pray for mercy, and God knew what His answer would be. We know that God doesn't do this for everyone, and we know that Hezekiah wasn't particularly deserving. But this story does illustrate that God occasionally approves of compromise (though His omniscience makes it different than the compromise we would practice).

At first, compromise will never feel like the right thing to do. By definition, compromise means "giving something up." If it were easy to give up, you wouldn't give it much thought, so compromise nearly always involves giving up something important to you. If it's important to you, it probably doesn't feel right.

The early church faced a difficult compromise where both sides felt that there was an important theological point worth defending.

In Acts 15, it is clear that there was a strong disagreement between two groups of early Christians. It is important to keep in mind that Jesus, all of His disciples, and all of the early Christians were Jewish. They tried to keep the entire Jewish law. Even though today we draw a distinction between Jews and Christians, the early church knew of no such difference. To be Christian meant to be Jewish; all Christians were Jewish.

So as non-Jewish people (Gentiles) began to become Christians, it was natural for them to assume that these Gentiles would keep the Jewish law. In a sense, they could only imagine that to convert to Christianity involved converting to Judaism as well.

In some ways, converting to Christianity was liberating for these Gentiles. They repented of their sin and believed in Christ. Converting to Judaism, however, proved quite difficult. It meant adopting the dietary laws and holidays, which means a significant change in lifestyle. But above all, it meant for men that they would become circumcised, no matter how old they were. Every male Christian up until the time of Acts 15 had been circumcised, because they were all Jewish. But now the church faced a difficult question—would they demand that Gentile men get circumcised? Would they demand that all Gentiles keep the Jewish dietary laws? Can you be a Christian without becoming Jewish?

We read of their answer in Acts 15:28-29: "It seemed good to the Holy Spirit and to us not to burden you with anything beyond the following requirements: You are to abstain from food sacrificed to idols, from blood, from the meat of strangled animals and from sexual immorality. You will do well to avoid these things."

In other words, the church decided on a compromise. The Jewish Christians realized that circumcision was an unbearable burden for Gentiles (in fact, the whole law is unbearable for anyone, as Paul makes clear in the book of Romans). But they still couldn't see themselves eating in "unclean" homes with Gentiles or fellowshipping with Christians who ate unclean food. So instead of the Gentiles obeying the whole Jewish law, they would observe a few key laws—not for their own sake, but for the sake of Jewish Christians who may want to eat in their homes or with them.

Scholars have a variety of responses to this story in Acts 15. Some believe that this compromise was not the best solution, and others think the whole story downplays the level of consternation that existed among these two ethnic groups in the early church. My purpose in telling the story here, however, is simply to point out that the Bible does allow for compromise as a possible solution to conflict. It is one among other positive options for relational change.

WHAT IT LOOKS LIKE IN MARRIAGE

Compromise is difficult in marriage because the need to compromise generally illustrates that the partners have differing values. Mike told me that his wife, Sharon, wants him to spend less time playing video games. (He loves the violent game, Halo.) His wife wishes that he would never play the game again, but she believes that is an unreasonable request. She thinks he has an unhealthy problem, though. Mike admits that he has played the game for as much as eight hours in a day, but generally, he plays two hours a day. He justifies this pastime by pointing out that he works from home, so he gets to spend more time in the house than most fathers. Two hours a day could easily be spent commuting. He also points out that if he watches TV with his wife (who spends two hours a day that way), she doesn't complain, and he doesn't have a problem with her pastime. He thinks she is pointing the finger unfairly at video games.

I asked Mike and Sharon what they think the chances are that they will both feel good about the amount of time he spends playing Halo. Immediately, they both knew they would never both feel good about whatever number they agree on. I think they are right, and the reason they won't reach this point is that they don't believe the other person holds the same values that they do. They are threatened by the thought that their partner rejects something they value.

What does Mike value about playing Halo? He values unwinding. He values recreation. He values entertainment and "vegging."

Which value does Sharon hold that makes her wish Mike would drop the game? She values time with the family. She values productivity. She values herself (being seen as important to Mike).

While Mike and Sharon may not come to a number of hours on Halo that they both feel good about, they can aim for another goal. Mike and Sharon can come to a point where they are convinced their partner shares the same values or at least validates the other person's value.

I asked Sharon, "Do you value Mike's need to unwind? Do you value his need for recreation? Do you value his need to 'veg'?" She said emphatically that she did.

I asked Mike, "Do you value time with the family? Do you value productivity? Do you value Sharon?" He convincingly said that he did.

This conversation about values is more productive than a conversation about hours spent on *Halo*. If Mike and Sharon had created a schedule with two hours of *Halo* a day, whatever suspicion they had that their partner did not share their values would have been "set in stone" and made painfully obvious. Writing out a schedule would have heightened their sense of defeat and threat.

Once Mike and Sharon are convinced that they share each other's values, they may still have a practical discussion about how many hours a day on *Halo* is acceptable. Or, they may not. Mike and Sharon agree that when he is playing *Halo*, she feels invisible to him. She fears that she doesn't matter, and she feels neglected. Even if Mike whittled down his *Halo* time to 10 minutes a day, she would resent that time as representative of personal rejection. On the other hand, Mike can find ways to express genuine concern for Sharon all day long. If he touches her every time he passes by, looks up at her every time she speaks, and helps whenever he senses a need, he will earn some serious game time. A 10-minute investment in attention to Sharon could buy him an hour of *Halo*.

I mean for this to sound ridiculous, but there is some truth in it. Love does not seek its own, so Mike should not have any selfish motive in paying attention to Sharon. But Mike shouldn't be oblivious to the fact that his attention to Sharon is the underlying issue, so he should address that rather than the time spent on Halo. It is possible that Mike and Sharon don't need a schedule or an agreed on number of hours as long as Mike connects with Sharon and demonstrates that she is his first priority. In doing this, he removes the threat that *Halo* represented.

But some couples may still need the schedule, or at least some ground rules. The important thing to keep in mind is that these parameters should still focus on values, rather than only on numbers or times of day. What can Mike do differently to demonstrate that

Sharon is his first priority? What can Sharon do differently to demonstrate that she believes in his need for recreation? This conversation may result in a number of hours a day, or it may result in some other creative decision that doesn't limit but only changes the relational dynamic such as:

- Mike could play in the same room as Sharon, so that she feels connected to him.
- He could decide to play only when he is the only person at home.
- Sharon could agree to play with him a couple times a week, as long as he agrees not to wipe her out.

What I am suggesting here is that the discussion revolve around values, rather than rules. This discussion may result in a change of behavior that both parties agree to, but that change will not feel like defeat. Instead, it will feel like a win-win situation because neither party fears that something they value is threatened. As both partners validate the other person's value, they find a way to work in new ways that demonstrate that agreement.

In the chapter on sacrifice, I cited Gottman's fourth relational principle. It has relevance to compromise as well. Gottman says, "The cornerstone of any compromise is the fourth principle of marriage—accepting influence."[62] Sometimes, letting your partner influence you means you sacrifice your own desires, change your mind about something or work out an intentional compromise. Gottman warns of the importance of compromise:

> In our long-term study of 130 newlywed couples, now in
> its eighth year, we have found that, even in the first few

months of marriage, men who allow their wives to influence them have happier marriages and are less likely
to divorce than men who resist their wives' influence.
Statistically speaking, when a man is not willing to share
power with his partner, there is an 81 percent chance that
his marriage will self-destruct.[63]

It is often said that when two people compromise, neither gets
their way. Since that is largely true, people are not completely pleased
with compromise. But, as Gottman's research shows, people are quite
unhappy when they get the sense that they cannot affect the other
person's decision-making.

WHAT IT LOOKS LIKE IN PARENTING

In the prior discussion on making a boundary, I expressed the
importance of consistency. Some parents may object to the concept
of compromise, saying that it is inconsistent. We have a rule in our
home that kids under 12 go to bed at 9:00 p.m. When my daughter,
Rebekah, asked if she could stay up until 10:00 to watch a movie, she
was obviously asking for an exception to a rule. If she didn't ask and
just did as she pleased, then I would have to discipline her. But if
she asks respectfully, and I agree, then I don't have to worry about
the issue of consistency. If an exception to a rule is clearly stated, it
doesn't mean that you are being inconsistent as a parent. We told
Rebekah she could watch the movie, and so we compromised our
rule. But we weren't inconsistent in disciplining her because there
was nothing to discipline.

Sometimes, however, kids make compromise impossible by their
own actions. If Rebekah had done as she pleased, rather than go to

---

63 Gottman, *The Seven Principles for Making Marriage Work*, 100.

bed, her behavior would have to be addressed. And if she asked to watch the movie but acted defiantly after we said "no," her attitude would also have to be addressed. The ability for a parent to compromise is diminished once the conflict begins.

My son's friend Nathan asked his father if he could stay the night at our house. His father said it wouldn't work out, and then Nathan, who was 13, started to argue with his dad. He said his dad's reason was stupid and that he could figure out a way to make it work. His dad's answer was wise. He said, "Nathan, I was able to change my mind at the beginning of this conversation and still be faithful to my duty as a father. If you had said, 'Yes, Dad, I believe there is a way to work this out if you would like to hear it,' then I might have been able to compromise. But you have made compromise impossible now because if I say yes, then I reward your disrespect."

Nathan's dad was right; compromise could have been fruitful at the beginning. Maybe the sleepover could have been arranged. But his dad's primary duty is to instruct; and once his son became disrespectful, the compromise would fail to instruct.

There are instances where compromise may resolve conflict without abrogating your responsibility as a parent. Parents often make rules that seem like they are based on right and wrong, but sometimes this distinction may be less clear. The way a child dresses, for instance, may disturb you, but it may not violate a clear biblical command. Sure, there is a clear biblical command to obey parents, so if you tell your child not to dress a certain way, it would violate scripture for them to do it anyway. But your revulsion to the way they dress may not really be addressed in scripture. You are probably tempted to find it somewhere in the Bible, but if you are honest with yourself, what you will find in scripture are principles for dress, but not detailed commands. These principles include modesty, submission, gender conformity, etc. But the Bible doesn't specifically say a boy can't have a Mohawk.

One way to resolve, or at least lighten, conflict in the home is to find areas of compromise, but you don't want to compromise on biblical commands. So try to find areas that are not clear biblical commands where you can compromise. By doing this, you will reserve the right to take a stronger stand in the areas that truly matter. As the parent, you have the right to enforce your rules, but you can make this easier for your kids by having fewer of them. Make them count. Emphasize the right things.

GETTING TO THE CORE OF COMPROMISE: BEHAVIOR, VALUES, BELIEFS, AND FEAR

People reach compromise easier if they begin with what they have in common. I have found that they generally have more in common than they think, even in regard to their present conflict. The chart below is helpful in finding that common ground. There are four concentric circles, with behavior on the outside. We normally talk about behavior because that is what we see. But as long as the discussion remains at the behavioral level, we remain at an impasse. People always do what they do for a reason. Behavior stems from values. These values are based on beliefs. Many of us can reach inside ourselves this far and see the beliefs that support the values that determine our behavior. But there is one even deeper, often hidden circle—fear.

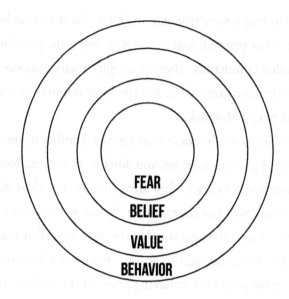

Consider the following conversation I had with a couple who came for marriage counseling. We began talking about spending habits (behavior) and ended up talking about fear.

Dan: "Janet, you spend more money on 'beauty' than your husband thinks is in the budget. Jerry, you wish Janet would spend less. What value are you holding on to?"

Jerry: "Well, I value good stewardship."

Janet: "I value good stewardship too!"

Jerry: "And you think a monthly manicure, pedicure, hair style, facial, and eyebrow wax is good stewardship?" [Not helpful]

Dan: "Janet, I assume you share Jerry's value of good stewardship. So let's frame the conversation a different way. Tell me why you spend this money on beauty, starting with 'I believe . . .'"

Janet: "I believe . . . um . . . other than that I should be able to spend my money how I want . . . that . . . we should look our best."

Jerry: "But there's got to be a point where you draw the line."

Dan: "Janet, let's try this one more way. Tell me why you pay this much attention to your appearance, starting with 'I fear . . . .'"

Janet: "I fear that I'm going to be old and unattractive."

Now this conversation may not immediately result in a dollar amount that both partners can agree on, but it will turn the discussion away from stewardship, which wasn't the real issue, and from a debate on where to draw the line on looking our best. Compromise can come. But first, Jerry needs to connect with the actual place of disagreement. Jerry and Janet don't disagree about stewardship or the philosophy of self-presentation. The real disagreement is that Jerry does not fear Janet becoming unattractive, but Janet does.

CHAPTER 9

REPENT

REPENTANCE IS A POWERFUL WAY to change your relationship
with others. Marie could repent of her own behaviors and attitudes
toward her mother and sister. She is frustrated with the two of them
for not cleaning up the bathroom, but perhaps she bears some responsibility for this situation as well. I can think of a variety of
things Marie may need to repent of.

Perhaps she has been rude. Maybe the relationship is strained
due to something deeper than the surface issue of the bathroom's
cleanliness. Her mother and sister may be using this opportunity to
provoke and expose "the way she treats them." It could be that they
feel justified in their refusal to clean because they see themselves as
victims of her negative attitude.

Perhaps Marie has been too passive. She may be able to repent
of enabling her sister and mother to develop an unhealthy lifestyle.
She might identify herself as overly passive and repent of this fear
of confrontation.

On the other hand, perhaps Marie has been too controlling. It
could be that her definition of a clean bathroom is unreasonable and
that no one could ever live up to her expectation. She feels disturbed

by the bathroom, and her sister and mother should want to validate her feelings. But the truth is, every relationship has a limit to the number of things you can be disturbed about. At some point, we must realize that maybe we get frustrated or angry too easily about too many things.

I don't know that any of these occasions for repentance are true for Marie, but it cannot hurt for her to use this occasion of conflict to do some soul-searching and to see what part of her soul God is trying to refine or shape. She could use this conflict to ask God the question found in Psalm 139:23-24, "Search me, God, and know my heart; test me and know my anxious thoughts. See if there is any offensive way in me, and lead me in the way everlasting."

DEFINITION OF "REPENTANCE"

"The recognition of wrong-doing and the decision to change."

Something in our human nature makes us always want to be right. Once, during a family dinner, my father-in-law stated some body of water was 40 degrees. Everyone around that table quickly and loudly began ridiculing that number. "It had to be warmer. Much warmer." Outnumbered, my father-in-law defended himself: "I meant Celsius!" Ever since, whenever my wife or I have been caught saying something erroneous we have retorted: "I meant Celsius." It's our shortcut for "I was right even though we all know I was wrong." But admitting guilt and repenting of wrong-doing may be the essential step to you getting "untrapped."

What if I don't have anything to repent of? The concept in this chapter does not apply strictly to turning from sin but to repairing the relationship in general. Sometimes repair is necessary, even when a specific sin cannot be identified. The word "repair" is useful because it doesn't imply blame, and it is forward thinking rather than focused on the past.

The idea of repair is preferable to the word "resolve." Too often, people try to resolve conflict but, depending on how resolution is defined, it is rarely possible. Usually people take the word "resolve" to mean that they come to an agreement. This agreement can include agreeing on who was wrong, who was at fault, or what should be done. But often, the best two people can hope to agree on is their commitment to one another. They can agree that they feel bad about how the conversation went and that they are resolved to love one another and to build each other up.

The ability to repair is vital to healthy relationships. Gottman stresses:

> In our research we actually have a technical name for what [successful couples] did. Probably unwittingly, they used a repair attempt. This name refers to any statement or action—silly or otherwise—that prevents negativity from escalating out of control. Repair attempts are the secret weapon of emotionally intelligent couples—even though many of these couples aren't aware that they are doing something so powerful. When a couple has a strong friendship, they naturally become experts at sending each other repair attempts and at correctly reading those sent their way.[64]

These repairs do not always have to include the words, "I'm sorry, I sinned." But there must be some sort of repair or turning toward one another. Without it, resentment builds. No doubt you have a

---

64 Gottman, *The Seven Principles for Making Marriage Work*, 22.

grudge list that contains many petty things. Why have these irrita-
tions remained in your memory if they are so petty? It is not the size
of the infraction we remember; it is the lack of repair that keeps it in
our memory. The effort for repair helps erase the injustice.

Pastor Tom Holladay writes about our ability to identify sin in
our lives. We can be blind to our own sin, and we are masters at self-
justification. Holladay compares the ability to identify sin to an op-
tometrist test.

> I'd like to do a different kind of test with you right now—
> not an "eye test," but an "I test." The more clearly you can
> read the two lines below, the more clearly you'll be able to
> apply Jesus' principle of judgment and mercy in your life.
>
> I HAVE SINNED.
>
> I AM FORGIVEN.[65]

How easy is it for you to really see what is in those two lines? The
beauty of the Gospel is that as we become increasingly aware of our
own wretchedness, we do not have to hide it, run from it, or fix it.
Christians embrace our wretchedness as an inescapable reality that
only serves to highlight the goodness of God. So to the extent that
we proclaim our sin, we also proclaim God's grace.

Holladay promises that coming to grips with our sin will also
transform our relationships:

> If you are willing first to ask [these questions] and then to
> listen for God's answers, three things will happen:
>
> • *You will be changed*; integrity will replace hypocrisy in
>   hidden areas of your life.

---

65 Holladay, *The Relationship Principles of Jesus*, 240.

- *Your relationships will be changed*; they'll breathe in the fresh air of mercy.
- *Those around you will be changed*; they will experience the loving, merciful touch of someone who knows how to remove a speck from a brother's or sister's eye.[66]

RULES FOR REPENTANCE

In counseling, I have found it helpful to identify five levels of apology. Some couples come for counseling and they are either so angry with each other or so inexperienced at apology that I have to lay out some ground rules, offer some examples, and then role play. It is amazing how difficult it is to utter an apology.

On the other hand, rarely will I hear what I would call "a perfect apology." It's worth perfecting yours, and abiding by these rules. For one thing, your apology will be received better. But don't perfect your apology just for pragmatic reasons or to gain a strategic advantage. The other benefit is that you will have a softer heart, you will be more repentant, and you will be humbler.

There is no right apology or wrong one. I always tell my clients, "Don't expect your spouse to have the perfect apology or even the right apology. Be satisfied you got one at all. That's a big first step."

Here are the five levels of apology, from least effective to most effective:
- "I'm sorry you . . . (I'm sorry you were so rude to me)."
- "I'm sorry if . . . (I'm sorry *if* I hurt your feelings)."

---

66 Holladay, *The Relationship Principles of Jesus*, 243.

- "I'm sorry but . . . (I'm sorry I acted so rudely, but I am at least partially justified because you made me so frustrated)."
- "I'm sorry it seemed . . . (I'm sorry it seemed like I was being a jerk)."
- "I'm sorry I . . . (I'm sorry I was rude to you)."

When I have my clients role play their apology, I don't make them use the fifth phrase above. That's because I want their apology to be authentic, a real offering, the best they can genuinely offer at the time. So I ask them to pick any of those phrases and make an apology. But I point out that these apologies have varied levels of effectiveness.

Whenever I use the word effective, I find it helpful to identify what effect we are aiming at. The effects we are aiming at in an apology are:

- That I will have a right relationship with God,
- That I will repent (change my actions in the future), and
- That the other person will be offered restoration in his/her relationship with me.

These are the only effects that are within our control. Many clients envision that their apology will be effective for other reasons. They are hoping:

- That you will apologize in return,
- That you will forgive them,
- That you will get off their back,
- That you will understand their position, and
- That you will realize they didn't really sin in the first place.

If these are any of the effects that you are hoping for, don't apologize. For one, none of these things are within your control. You cannot make someone believe something or understand something. You cannot make someone repair the relationship. You don't get to tell the other person what to repent for until you repent yourself. And you can wait till tomorrow. Henry Cloud speaks of the way repentance is a catalyst for maturity. He writes:

> The reverse side of assigning blame is taking ownership. When we take ownership for what happens in our lives, we are empowered to make change. Ownership frees us to do something, make plans, tackle hurtful situations, and right wrongs. People who take charge of their lives are active people with real initiative. Ownership also provides freedom. You are no longer a slave to the past, to false hopes, to wishing someone else would change, or to discouragement and passivity. You are free to take risks and to test-drive some possible solutions.[67]

The ability to take ownership of what we have done wrong is a sign of "growing up" and is vital for social and spiritual maturity.

DEFENSE AND ACCUSATION: THE NEGATIVE COUSINS OF REPENTANCE

Often, when God is giving us the opportunity to see our sin and repent, we react defensively instead. Being defensive is our nature; it's what Adam did in the garden when God called him out on his sin. Adam blamed his weakness on "the woman You gave me." It is easy to understand why we are defensive—because we can always find a shred of truth with which to justify ourselves. Gottman paints a picture of defensiveness in a story with a woman named Cynthia who argued with her husband about washing the car.

> It is no surprise, considering how nasty her husband is being, that Cynthia defends herself. She points out that she

---

67 Cloud, *What to Do When You Don't Know What to Do*, 45.

doesn't get her car washed as often as he thinks. She explains that it's more difficult physically for her to wash her car herself than it is for him to wash his truck. Although it's understandable that Cynthia would defend herself, research shows that this approach rarely has the desired effect. The attacking spouse does not back down or apologize. This is because defensiveness is really a way of blaming your partner. You're saying, in effect, "The problem isn't me, it's you." Defensiveness just escalates the conflict, which is why it's so deadly.[68]

Putting the other person on guard is the opposite of what we want in our relationships. That's because protection is the opposite of intimacy.

I was visiting a good friend of mine at his office. We were in the middle of a serious discussion when another friend walked by, saw that I was visiting, and came to chat as well. He ended up dominating the time. Because this was not the first time my friend Joseph had taken over a conversation, I felt compelled to address this with him. Normally, even the most mature people have a difficult time hearing criticism, so I braced myself for the confrontation.

I said to him, "Joseph, when I was talking to Todd the other day, you came in and acted like the conversation was just beginning. This seemed insensitive." Joseph's response showed his maturity in the area of repentance. He said, "Yes . . . that is what I do. I'm sorry."

Unfortunately, because of our inherent pride ever since Adam's fall, we do not normally repent so easily. More commonly, when someone tells us that we have sinned, we:

- Tell the other person how they have sinned against us,

---

68 Gottman, *The Seven Principles for Making Marriage Work*, 32.

- Say, "Don't be so sensitive" (minimize the other person's feelings),
- Place the blame on someone else,
- Defend or justify ourselves by saying we had to do what we did,
- Deny that we did anything wrong, or
- Overreact, saying that the other person hates us or that this signifies the end of the friendship.

WHAT REPENTANCE LOOKS LIKE IN THE BIBLE

We don't have an instance in the Bible where God repents, of course, since God is perfect. But there are plenty of examples of people who repented. We read in the book of Judges that the nation of Israel had slipped into idolatry, as they were in the habit of doing. Because of this idolatry, the Lord allowed the people to be sold into slavery under a neighboring nation called Ammon. We read:

The Ammonites also crossed the Jordan to fight against Judah, Benjamin and Ephraim; Israel was in great distress. Then the Israelites cried out to the LORD, "We have sinned against you, forsaking our God and serving the Baals." The LORD replied, "When the Egyptians, the Amorites, the Ammonites, the Philistines, the Sidonians, the Amalekites, and the Maonites oppressed you and you cried to me for help, did I not save you from their hands? But you have forsaken me and served other gods, so I will no longer save you. Go and cry out to the gods you have chosen. Let them save you when you are in trouble!" But the Israelites said to the LORD, "We have sinned. Do with us whatever you think best, but please rescue us now." Then they got rid of the foreign gods among them and served the LORD. And he could bear Israel's misery no longer (Judg. 10:9-16).

It is important to notice how repentance included a verbal admission of wrong doing and a change in future action. Though we may not always be guilty of what the other person is accusing us and though we may not be the primary responsible party in every conflict, we almost always have something of which to repent. That's because we are so thoroughly corrupt in our sinful nature. John reminds us, "If we claim to be without sin, we deceive ourselves and the truth is not in us" (1 Jn. 1:8).

The prodigal son provides an example of what I would call "the perfect apology." It's no surprise that the response would be perfect, since it is actually the words of Jesus in the form of a parable. So through this parable, we can learn from Jesus how to make a good apology. The prodigal son says, "Father, I have sinned against heaven and against you. I am no longer worthy to be called your son" (Lk. 15:21).

In this rather short apology, we see several vital elements of the perfect apology. Notice the key elements of the prodigal son's apology:

- He admits that he has sinned.
- He says he sinned against God and his father.
- He understands the consequences of his sin.
- He exhibits humility.
- He offers repentance (a promise to change).

In the book of Daniel, we read about a man who became an expert at repentance—King Nebuchadnezzar. I say "expert" because he had so many occasions of sin and repentance that he perfected the art!

First we read about the three men who refused to bow down to the image of himself. Nebuchadnezzar threw Shadrach, Meshach, and Abednego in a fiery furnace because of their obstinacy. But after the men survived the furnace, he said:

> Praise be to the God of Shadrach, Meshach and Abednego, who has sent his angel and rescued his servants! They trusted in him and defied the king's command and were willing to give up their lives rather than serve or worship any god except their own God. Therefore I decree that the people of any nation or language who say anything against the God of Shadrach, Meshach, and Abednego be cut into pieces and their houses be turned into piles of rubble, for no other god can save in this way" (Dan. 3:28-29).

The lesson about repentance had to be relearned, however, because Nebuchadnezzar had an almost identical change of heart when the prophet Daniel warned the king about his pride. The king fancied himself as the most powerful man in the world, and as a result, God drove Nebuchadnezzar out of the kingdom to live like a wild animal. But again, the king repented. We read:

> At the end of that time, I, Nebuchadnezzar, raised my eyes toward heaven, and my sanity was restored. Then I praised the Most High; I honored and glorified him Who lives forever. his dominion is an eternal dominion; his kingdom endures from generation to generation.

All the peoples of the earth are regarded as nothing. He does as He pleases with the powers of heaven and the peoples of the earth. No one can hold back His hand or say to Him: "What have you done?" (Dan. 4:34-35).

In Genesis 33, we find a touching story of profound repentance. Jacob and Esau were twins with a Bible-sized rivalry. By tricking their father, Isaac, Jacob stole the blessing and the inheritance to which Esau was entitled. For years, Jacob avoided Esau, assuming that his brother would kill him if he got the chance.

When he learned that a meeting with his twin was imminent, Jacob sent gifts of livestock and grain ahead, hoping these things would put Esau in a better mood. This was a strategic move, not necessarily a sign that his heart had changed.

But we read that Jacob bowed down seven times before his brother as a sign of repentance. It seems that Esau's heart had already been prepared to accept to apology because he came and kissed Jacob, and they both wept. This story is a beautiful example of repentance and forgiveness and an early promise in the Bible of relational repair.

WHAT REPENTANCE LOOKS LIKE IN MARRIAGE

We have already seen that marriage serves as one of God's most effective tools for making us holy. That's why Thomas writes, "Couples don't fall out of love so much as they fall out of repentance."[69] In the event that your friends and coworkers are failing effectively to help you see your sin, have no fear. Your spouse will do the job quite well. Your spouse is better positioned than anyone else to see your faults, and, hopefully, he or she will remember that you have the same clear vantage point as well. Rather than induce fear, defensiveness, or resentment, this thought should produce relief.

It is a relief to know that God has not left us without the means to fulfill the glorious purpose to which He has assigned us. Les and Leslie Parrott speak of the important role that repentance and

---

69 Thomas, *Sacred Marriage,* 96.

forgiveness play in marriage: "Forgiveness lies at the heart of marriage. Two people living together, day after day, stumbling over each other's beings, are bound to cause pain, sometimes innocently, sometimes not. And if forgiveness is not given to cleanse the marriage soul, condemnation hovers over the relationship.[70]

It is in the microcosm of marriage that the drama of God's redemptive history with humanity is acted out. Daily, we get a reminder in marriage that undeserving people are showered with undeserved grace and that this is one of life's greatest pleasures.

Far more important than fixing your faults is the priority of fixing your apologies. That should be a relief because the prospect of fixing your faults is dim. So if you can perfect your apology, you will have achieved a scandalous shortcut! And that is the scandal of the Gospel that sinners would be saved by grace (and not by works). Les and Leslie Parrot write:

> All couples need a healing mechanism, a way to turn a new page in marriage, and knowing how and when to say you're sorry can make a big difference . . . An apology may not be a literal "I'm sorry"; it may be giving gifts, sharing an evening out, or simply taking a quiet walk together. The point is that a sincere apology, whatever its form, leaves the couple with a renewed closeness and a relieved feeling that all is well."[71]

Developing such a mechanism is not difficult. The difficult part is cultivating the heart, for out of the abundance of the heart, the mouth speaks. If repentance is in your heart, your words will betray that fact no matter how clumsily you emit your apology.

---

70 Parrott and Parrott, *Saving Your Marriage Before it Starts*, 145.
71 Parrott and Parrott, *Saving Your Marriage Before it Starts*, 93.

Repentance will almost always follow an emotional appeal. Unless you have exceptional self-reflection and are often tuned into the promptings of the Holy Spirit, God will use the other people in your life to make you aware that you have sinned. That's why it's extremely important when your friends or loved ones appeal to you emotionally that you do not react defensively. Don't let your first thought be to explain or justify yourself. When others tell you they are frustrated or upset, let your first thought be, "What can I apologize for?" When you make an emotional appeal to your spouse, isn't this the response you are hoping for?

Lynette came into my office saying that her husband, Alex, always thinks he is better than she is. It is a difficult thing for a man to apologize for "always thinking he is better than she is." The charge is too global and too vague. So I asked her to tell me one story.

Lynette said that last week they were talking about their bills, and she said she was worried they had mounting debt. Alex said, "I'll take care of it; you don't know what's going on." Now this is a specific instance where someone can connect and repent. So I asked Alex to apologize.

Alex's response was typical for many couples who are struggling with repentance as a way of relating. He said, "You don't even know our password for our online banking!" Because of our fallen nature, apologies don't come naturally to us. Satan used Adam's pride to tempt him, saying that Adam would become like God if he ate of the forbidden fruit. So we have a lot of relearning to do.

I wrote on my whiteboard the four levels of apology and asked Alex to finish one of the sentences. First, I explained that "I'm sorry I . . . " would be the most effective, and "I'm sorry you . . . " would be the least effective. Alex impressively overcame his pride and said, "I'm sorry I made you feel stupid."

This was a great apology because it connected with how she was feeling. And Alex took personal responsibility, implying that he had sinned. Even if Alex still believed that his wife was not involved enough in the finances, he could still apologize for how he made her feel. No matter how justified he is in thinking he knows more about money, he cannot deny that somehow his actions contributed to how she was feeling. So apologizing for how you made someone feel is a great place to start. It is undeniable that the other person felt that way and that you helped cause it. You can apologize for that.

There are more mature places to get to in repentance, however. Alex could also say, "I'm sorry I have not valued your thoughts and feelings about money." This apology takes even more responsibility for what Alex has done and expresses more clearly how he can change.

In the first couple years of my marriage, I grew weary feeling that I was always the first person to repent. I remember having an argument and thinking, "I am willing to repent and get this conversation moving in the right direction, but I want to see how long it takes her—if ever. Why does it always have to be me to go first?"

If you're ever tempted to try an experiment for relational change, don't. And if you sense you are in the middle of one, stop. These sarcastic relational "experiments" serve to give us facts that support our theory. The outcome of your experiment is predetermined; you will most definitely gather all of the information you need to validate your anger or judgment. You don't need this, and it won't facilitate relational change. Just determine now that you will be the first to apologize, every time, even as long as the relationship endures. Rather than seeing this as a victim, count yourself lucky that God has gifted you with the strength and wisdom to see what is needed and to willingly offer it.

WHAT REPENTANCE LOOKS LIKE IN PARENTING

Marriage is not the only drama where God has designed us to experience the redemption of sin, forgiveness, repentance, and grace. Josh McDowell explains:

> The ability to admit mistakes and ask forgiveness is apparently rare among Christian parents. A survey of church kids revealed that 37 percent of the kids surveyed—more than one in three—say they seldom or never hear their parents admit to being wrong or having done wrong. Presumably, even fewer ask for forgiveness from their children. No wonder our kids have trouble admitting their mistakes! No wonder they have trouble identifying with their parents! No wonder they struggle with self-esteem—their parents are apparently perfect![72]

As a parent, if you fail to identify sin in your life and repent in your relationship with your children, you rob them of two things. First, you rob them of justice. Second, you rob them of a learning opportunity, where they see you model repentance.

Recently my wife told our four-year-old that she was being disobedient and that she would have to go to time-out. Four minutes later, when she returned to us, Leah was in hysterical tears and said to my wife, "Say you're sorry."

72 McDowell, *The Father Connection*, 150.

My wife said, "I did not do anything wrong, Leah. I am not going to say I'm sorry."

Leah continued shedding her out-of-control tears. My wife and I could tell that she was heartbroken over her sin and wanted restoration, but we could not offer that restoration by apologizing to her. Eventually, we realized when Leah spoke next that she had misspoken and was reaching for the right words to say.

She screamed, "Say I forgive you!"

My wife, of course, offered forgiveness with hugs and kisses. Something in us longs for, and is desperate for, reconciliation. We don't always know the right words to say or exactly how to express what we have done wrong, but we profoundly feel that reconciliation is necessary and that it is currently lacking.

REPENTANCE IS A DISPLAY OF GOD'S GLORY

I know a father who asked his three-year-old son to "pinky promise" every morning that he would be good. When I heard about this, I suggested that they modify this promise. I offered that they could promise that if either of them sinned, they would seek resolution and forgiveness. I don't want to ask my children to promise to be perfect. One reason is that I don't believe they can keep the promise. Also, the promise has no backup plan should my kids fail to live up to it. I'm not sure that this is what God asks us to promise. Finally, the promise to be perfect doesn't leave much room for God to display His glorious character.

The seventeenth century philosopher Gottfried Wilhelm Leibniz argued that God made the best of all possible worlds. I think Leibniz is right. God could have made a world without sin, but He didn't. Why didn't He? The only options are that He either couldn't do it, didn't know how it was going to turn out, or didn't think it was best. If you believe God is all-powerful and all-knowing, then you must choose the last option—God, knowing that the world would have sin, and able to prevent it from doing so, chose to make a world that would have sin because this was best.

How could a world with sin possibly be the best possible world? That entirely depends on what you are trying to accomplish. If the goal was human happiness, then perhaps God failed. If God's goal was peace, then He clearly failed. If the goal was equality, then God did not make the best possible world. So God clearly had a different goal in mind, where a sinful world was the best possible one to accomplish His purpose.

Paul tells us this purpose in Romans 1:20, "For since the creation of the world God's invisible qualities—his eternal power and divine nature—have been clearly seen, being understood from what has been made . . . " God's purpose was to display his attributes. The history of the world is a story where God is the main character, and the setting allows Him to display His qualities. Psalm 19:1 says, "The heavens declare the glory of God; the skies proclaim the work of his hands."

REPENTANCE AS AN IMPORTANT EXAMPLE

In Romans 6, Paul makes the case that where sin is abundant, grace is abundant. He asks, then, if that is true, shouldn't we sin all the more in order to let grace be even more evident? Obviously not! God takes no pleasure in sin, and we should never desire to sin or to be sinned against. But given the inevitability of sin, we can rejoice that it is an opportunity for the character of God to be displayed in us.

If my daughter sins against me, I get to forgive her. And when I forgive her, I reflect the character of God. God's forgiveness is displayed. James tells us to consider all trials as pure joy (Jas. 1:2). Sin puts a trial upon a relationship, and it is never fun, but there is one cause for joy—we get to see the face of Christ in one another as we extend grace.

I thought of this when Ella, a wife and mother of two teenagers, came for counseling with her husband because they had been arguing quite a bit lately. She said, "Unfortunately, the kids are exposed to this." It is unfortunate in many ways.

I told Ella, "I know eternal optimism can be irritating, so forgive me for saying this. I don't wish a fight for you or your kids, but it's not completely unfortunate. Your kids will learn healthy ways to resolve conflict by watching your example. This will prepare them for future conflict, which will inevitably come."

I would never plan to sin against my kids in order to teach some lesson on repentance and forgiveness. But I would hate to send them into the world unprepared to deal with conflict because they had the unfortunate lot to be stuck with perfect parents. So, thankfully, there are plenty of occasions where I end up sinning against them anyway, and these moments serve as a divine example where I can let them return the favor of forgiveness that I also give to them. Rather than just expecting them to ask for forgiveness when they sin against me, I can model what God is looking for when I sin against them.

WHAT TO EXPECT OF OTHERS

When we ask for forgiveness, we generally want something from the other person. We are implicitly asking them to absolve us of guilt, promise to forget the incident, continue to love us, or say, and "I forgive you." It's important with this option of repentance to remember that the other person's response is outside of your control.

I asked a group of parents to discuss what kind of response they expected from their kids when they asked them for forgiveness. Kelly said she expects her children to say, "I forgive you."

I asked her, "What if they sound like they don't mean it when they say it?"

And she said, "I make them say it again."

"What if they refuse?" I asked.

She said she would tell them that they're mean and show them how sad she is that they didn't forgive her.

Kelly's strategy sounds like a recipe for disaster to me. For one thing, she is "making" her kids do something she can't "make" them do. This means she is under an illusion of control which she doesn't actually have. Living under that illusion means she is in for a power struggle with her kids. Eventually, she will figure out that she can't make them say it, and she will have to give up, showing her weakness. But before she gets to that point she will likely try a variety of manipulative strategies, like appealing to her emotions (telling them they are mean).

How she feels about their unforgiveness is somewhat irrelevant to whether it is a sin for them not to forgive. If the primary role of parenting is instruction, her goal is not to make children who make her feel happy but who obey God. It would be wiser to tell her kids that they are being unforgiving, and this is wrong.

But this leads to another reason Kelly's strategy is bound to fail. She expects to be able to tell the difference between sincere forgiveness and insincere forgiveness. I am not confident of my ability to do this. To be sure, if a child says. "I forgive you," in a sarcastic tone, we might say, "You sound sarcastic. That is disrespectful." But what's the point of trying to figure out if the forgiveness is sincere or not. It seems that offering the words, "I forgive you," is a great discipline, regardless of the emotion behind it.

If forgiveness is an act of the will more than an act of the emotion (and I think that it is), then saying, "I forgive you," is an obedient act of the will. I trust that the emotion will follow the obedience with time. And conversely, I trust that emotions of unforgiveness will follow disobedience with time as well.

There is a further reason why Kelly's drive to hear those words, "I forgive you," is misguided. By requiring her kids to say something that they might not really mean, she risks hardening their hearts. Certainly, saying, "I forgive you," is an act of obedience to God, and it is healthy for her children to do it. But whenever Kelly requires her child to do something that Kelly can't control, she has made it more likely to harden her child's heart.

If Kelly says to her daughter, "Say, 'I forgive you,' but her daughter refuses, then she gets away with disobedience. Her daughter learns that it is possible to sin without consequences, other than mom getting upset. Of course, Kelly could say, "Tell me you forgive me, or you will get a spanking," but is this really the direction she wants to go with this apology?

It would be better for Kelly to say something like, "I am sorry for what I did. I would appreciate it if you would forgive me. It would be healthy for you to tell me you forgive me. If you don't forgive me, there will be bitterness in your heart, and that is not healthy for you."

Once, my wife asked my six-year-old daughter, Rebekah, to apologize, so she said in a sarcastic, angry tone, "I'm SORRY!" My two-year old daughter picked up on the apparent insincerity and said, "That's not 'sorry'; 'sorry' is this kind . . . " And then she said in the sweetest voice, "Sorry."

Though my daughter was perceptive and correct, we also often make the mistake of expecting the other person's apology to be perfect or better than we got. I encourage you to settle for a "good enough" apology. For some people, the concept is so new, the relationship is so damaged, or the self is so large, that offering an apology is harder than we imagine. Resist the temptation to criticize someone for apologizing. They will get the message that apologies don't work or don't pay off.

If the apology seems less than authentic, we should resist the tendency to say, "You're not really sorry." This is unfair because you cannot know for sure how the other person feels. It is a double accusation because it not only implies the other person is unrepentant, but also that they are a liar. If you are really offended by the apology or doubtful of its sincerity, you could say, "I feel uncertain about that apology." This is an emotional appeal. In some cases, that may be instructive and helpful, but in others, it may be asking a bit more than the relationship can handle.

Having a gauge for what the relationship can handle or what one can reasonably expect from the relationship at a particular stage is important. Many of the things we expect are justifiable, realistic, and reasonable. But we can't reasonably expect to have a perfect relationship today. That is, after all, why God has given us a lifetime for our sanctification (perfection). Any relationship that prompted you to read this book is important enough to you that you will be investing in it for years or a lifetime.

It was very liberating for me one day, when I had a discouraging argument with my wife early on in our marriage, that I realized, "This doesn't have to get fixed today." I wished that she was more patient. In fact, I couldn't handle the thought of 50 years of marriage without that changing. I was adamant that she had to change in order for us to have a successful relationship for the next 50 years. And then I realized—that means we have 50 years to work on it!

Still not very encouraged, in my mind I compromised and thought, even if we had to work on it for five more years, that would be acceptable. Then we could have 45 years with the problem solved.

We need to take the long view in relationships. Otherwise, we wouldn't be able to choose one of the nine options for relational change. Without the long view, we will be tempted to cover all nine options in every conflict. If every conflict represented the totality of the relationship, we would have to teach or leave every time and would never consider listening, doing nothing, or sacrificing.

We are also tempted, sometimes, to ask, "How do I know you are not going to do it again?" This is a dangerous question for several reasons:

- My wife can*not* know this, since it looks into the future.
- What's more, my wife and I both know that, in all likelihood, I will do it again, since I am a wretch of a sinner, and the things that bother her most are the things I keep on doing.
- But most of all, it's a mistake to ask because it is not the purpose of an apology.

An apology is a repair in the relationship. It is an offering for friendship, an outstretched hand, an olive branch. It is not a guarantee of the future, but it can be a guarantee of the current condition of one's heart.

CONCLUSION

THE MAIN THING: ACTING INTENTIONALLY

THE NEXT TIME YOU FACE a conflict, it may be difficult to decide which of these nine options for relational change you should follow. There is not a simple answer to that question. You may not even remember all nine options when a conflict arises. That's OK. There is probably not a right answer for what you should do, but the important thing is that you become intentional about your relationships. Act with purpose.

For example, if you put this book down and someone you love says, "Glad to see you finally finished reading that thing! Now you might actually get the help you need," what would you do? On a former day you might have done one of these things:

- Said something sarcastic. But now you might be intentional about teaching, "Our relationship also needs work."

- Gotten angry. But now you can make an intentional decision to make an emotional appeal like, "I feel hurt because it seems like you are accusing me."

- Said nothing. But now you can decide to listen: "Tell me more about this; how do you feel about our relationship?"

- Played the victim. But now you can make an intentional sacrifice. You can say to yourself, "I can take that; I don't need to be perfect in their eyes."

- Ignored the other person. But now you can purposely decide not to respond.

- Stormed out. But now you can intentionally decide to leave the room, cool off, and think about how to respond.

- Made a punishing remark. But now you can decide to make a boundary: "I choose not to respond to rude remarks."

- Bargained: "I will improve if you do." But now you can purposefully work toward compromise.

- Been defensive. But now you can intentionally choose to repent: "I'm sorry, I have made things difficult. I hope this book will help."

Overall, it does not matter much which of these options you choose. What matters more is that you no longer act passively or impulsively, but strategically. You have a way of deciding how you are going to act; a clear goal that you are trying to accomplish. You know there are multiple paths to getting to that point, and you are able to act on purpose. It is now my hope that you will:

- Be more aware of how you tend to react in the midst of conflict,

- Take control of how you relate and be more intentional, and

- Evaluate what your strategy was, how it worked, and how it could have been better.

YOUR ACTION PLAN

You can begin by evaluating yourself and the strategy you have normally **followed in the past.** Ask yourself:

- In the past, which of these nine options have I normally used?
- Which of the "negative cousins" have I also practiced?
- Which of these nine positive options are new skills that I need to develop?

And the next time you see **conflict on the horizon,** you feel your pulse start to rise, and you fear that you will be trapped, ask yourself:

- Which of these nine options do I intend to pursue?
- What is in the best interest of the other person?

Then, **after conflict,** when you look back, ask yourself:

- Which of these nine options did I end up doing? Or was it not really listed here and more likely to be found on the "negative cousin" chart?

BIBLIOGRAPHY

Augsburger, David. *Caring Enough to Confront.* Scottsdale: Herald Press, 1983.

Cline, Foster, and Jim Fay. *Parenting with Love and Logic.* Colorado Springs: NavPress Publishing, 2006.

Cloud, Henry, and John Townsend. *Boundaries.* Grand Rapids: Zondervan, 1992.

Cloud, Henry, and John Townsend. *Boundaries in Marriage.* Grand Rapids: Zondervan, 2002.

Crabb, Larry. *The Marriage Builder.* Grand Rapids: Zondervan, 1992.

Crabb, Larry. *Connecting.* Nashville: Word Books, 1997.

Dobson, James. *Love Must be Tough.* Carol Stream: Tyndale, 1996.

Gottman, John. *The Seven Principles for Making Marriage Work.* New York: Three Rivers Press, 1999.

Gottman, John. *The Relationship Cure.* New York: Three Rivers Press, 2002.

Holladay, Tom. *The Relational Principles of Jesus.* Grand Rapids: Zondervan, 2008.

McDowell, Josh. *Right vs. Wrong Curriculum*. Nashville: Thomas Nelson, 1994.

McDowell, Josh. *The Father Connection*. Nashville: B&H Publishing Group, 2008.

Parrott, Leslie, and Les Parrott. *Saving Your Marriage Before it Starts*. Grand Rapids: Zondervan, 2006.

Siegel, Daniel, and Mary Hartzell. *Parenting From the Inside Out*. New York: Jeremy Tarcher/Penguin, 2003.

Sittser, Gerald. *Love One Another*. Downers Grove: IVP Books, 2008.

Thomas, Gary. *Sacred Marriage*. Grand Rapids: Zondervan, 2000.

Tripp, Tedd. *Shepherding a Child's Heart*. Wapwallopen: Shepherds Press, 1995.

For more information about

Daniel Nehrbass
and
UnTrapped
please visit:

daniel@nightlight.org

www.danielnehrbass.com

www.facebook.com/daniel.nehrbass.5

For more information about
AMBASSADOR INTERNATIONAL
please visit:

www.ambassador-international.com
@AmbassadorIntl
www.facebook.com/AmbassadorIntl

If you enjoyed this book, please consider leaving us a review on
Amazon, Goodreads, or our website.